Strangeways 1990
A serious disturbance

Nicki Jameson and Eric Allison

with a foreword by
Michael Mansfield QC

'A serious disturbance broke out inside the prison at about
11.00am this morning amongst convicted prisoners in the chapel.'
Home Office press statement, 1 April 1990

IMPERIALISM

First Published 1995
Larkin Publications
BCM Box 5909, London WC1N 3XX

The authors:
Nicki Jameson is editor of Prisoners' Fightback
in *Fight Racism! Fight Imperialism!*
Eric Allison is a former Strangeways prisoner.

Photographs:
Ged Murray: pages 16, 28, 42, 50, 53, 55, 58, 61,
69, 70, 76, 83, 90, 106, 117, 118, 128, 159
Karen Minnitt: page 143

British Library Cataloguing in Publication Data
A catalogue record is available for this book from the British Library.

ISBN 0905400 18 6

Designed and typeset in Perpetua and Legacy by Boldface 0171 253 2014
Printed in Great Britain by BPC Wheatons Ltd, Exeter.

Contents

Acknowledgements

We would like to thank the following for their assistance:

First and foremost, prisoners who were present at the Strangeways uprising and who have provided material without which this book could never have been written: **Barry Morton, David Bowen, Alan Lord, Tony Bush, John Hughes, Paul Taylor, Mark Williams** and **Ian Allen**.

Other prisoners and ex-prisoners who have provided material, advice or help: Andy Russell, Paul Ross, Jimmy Morrison, John McGranaghan, Stephen Windsor, Peter Jordan, Tony Kavanagh, Mark Stoner-Seed, Andrzy Jakubczyk and, in particular, John Bowden.

Others who helped with material, background information or support: Vicky King (Prisoners' Advice Service), Andrew Green (Conviction), Adam Sampson (Prison Reform Trust), Alex Hodson (London Anarchist Black Cross), Vera Baird (Tooks Court Chambers), Debra Coles (Inquest), David Pocock and Dorothy Sheridan (Mass Observation), Mike Lodge (Bimpson Lodge solicitors), Professor Rod Morgan (Bristol University), Ged Murray and John Sutton.

The members and supporters of Manchester and Bradford Revolutionary Communist Group branches in April 1990, who translated the RCG's support for the prison struggle into practical activity; the Editorial Board of *Fight Racism! Fight Imperialism!*, particularly Carol Brickley and David Reed, for their help in structuring and producing this book, and all the comrades who helped with proof-reading and administration.

For Terry O'Halloran
who sadly didn't live to see it.

Foreword

The images of prison life conjured up by the comedy *Porridge* or the soap *Cell Block H* constantly mask the true iniquity of a system maintained still by an attitude of mind best reflected in the present Home Secretary. Despite universal condemnation from all quarters over the glib assertions that 'prison works' he has continued with his programme of longer sentences, more prisons and younger inmates. On top of this is the intention, initially denied, to privatise, with the inevitable consequences that have been felt in the Health Service, Education, Employment, Housing and now Transport.

This book provides a timely antidote and makes a vital contribution to the continuing campaign for change. It does so because it has the insight of an insider and because it tells a story so far untold in untrammelled fashion. It is easy to forget the extent of the disturbances which touched over 20 gaols in 1990 and led to the Woolf Inquiry. The public memory, so tainted by media muckraking, undoubtedly categorises the prisoners as 'rioters' and 'troublemakers'. The politicians who see no votes in prison reform and who scramble for the law-and-order high-ground demand new legislation, new offences, harsher penalties for prison riot and mutiny. In all of this the causes are submerged and lost in the quagmire of retribution. Those who have constantly warned of explosion in a system overheating by numbers alone have been ignored.

The trials that ensued did not embrace the real issues of policy that lie behind prison conditions but concentrated instead upon who did what to whom. One trial prior to Strangeways did do so – the Risley 54. All were acquitted, yet little or no attention was paid to their historic struggle for justice both in prison and in the courts.

Currently a similar preoccupation with effects rather than causes can be discerned – breaches of security; the number of disturbances (according to the Home Office in January 1995 running at more than 140 per year over the last three years); the amount of damage (£27.9 million for 1990/91).

Prisoners are better placed than anyone else to know what is wrong. It's not just about prison populations (the UK still leads the field, particularly those on remand); about overcrowding above European standards; about integral sanitation; about the dimensions of prison cells which remain unchanged.

More importantly it's about human rights and regimes. We have to rethink penal policy, the need for prisons, the kind of prisons required and the way in which they operate. Unless prisoners are treated as human beings and not disposable numbers; are given respect and dignity, and not treated as animals to be broken to the point of submission, there will be no progress into the next century. All regimes must recognise basic rights of access (families, loved ones, lawyers) at reasonable times for reasonable periods in reasonable conditions; rights of privacy and association; rights to reasonable resources for education, recreation and exercise; rights relating to personal possessions, clothing and food.

Michael Mansfield QC
February 1995

Introduction

'Less than three hours after arriving I was subjected to an unprovoked and vicious assault by approximately ten prison officers, most of whom were in a drunken condition. I was punched, kicked, headbutted, stripped naked and dragged through a gauntlet of warders to a strong-box cell. This, I was later to discover, was the standard introduction of the 'subversive' prisoner to the D3 unit. X-rays later revealed that I had suffered a badly fractured rib and my body was covered with multiple bruising.' *Prisoner at Winson Green 1989*

'I was again given a new cell-mate, who had not washed for some time and had no intention of washing. I asked to be removed from my cell for personal hygiene. On the way to the block I heard officers saying "We got the bastard!" and realised they had been baiting me all along. On arrival in the segregation unit...there was a large number of heavy-set men waiting for me. They told me to get in the cell and keep my mouth shut. I asked for my toiletries, letters and radio...four or five then entered my cell...They formed a half circle around me and stated I was on my own down here and I get whatever they want to give me..."so you just shut your black mouth and maybe you might get your food and we might remember to exercise you".' *Leicester 1994*

'[My mother] was eventually allowed in to see me but only after being delayed at the gatelodge for over an hour. When the visit did eventually take place it was under the most intimidating conditions imaginable, ie in an eight foot by eight foot 'room' with two staff present throughout the visit. This was in flagrant breach of Home Office regulations as I'm not on high-risk visits.' *Belmarsh 1992*

Outside every prison in England and Wales there is a notice which reads:

> 'Her Majesty's Prison Service serves the public by keeping in custody those committed by the courts. Our duty is to look after them with humanity and to help them lead law abiding lives in custody and after release.'

That is the official version: that offenders are sent to prison *as* a punishment, that loss of liberty *is* the punishment. But it is far from being the whole story and everybody concerned in the prison system – staff, governors, bureaucrats and the prisoners themselves – knows that, except for those few white-collar middle-class criminals who go straight to open prisons, punishment continues to be meted out throughout the sentence in many different forms, some physical, some psychological.

Brutal prisons are an integral part of the repressive apparatus of the British state, together with an increasingly well-armed paramilitary police force and a range of ever more draconian laws (the most recent being the 1994 Criminal Justice Act) which attempt to criminalise all forms of effective dissent. Imprisonment is part of the big stick, the threat, both to conscious political dissenters and to the mass of the 'undeserving poor', should they in any way step out of line or question their lot.

There are many myths peddled about the prison population and one of the biggest is that it is made up almost entirely of killers, rapists, 'terrorists' and drugs dealers. In fact, only a fifth of prisoners are serving time for anything involving violence and the overwhelming majority of prisoners, (including many of that fifth), are in gaol simply because they are working class and poor. And, as the divide between the richest and poorest people in Britain continues to widen, prisons are filling to bursting point. Their purpose is to maintain a degree of control by punishing those who enter and scaring those who remain outside.

Among people who have never been in gaol and have no relatives or friends there, ignorance of what goes on behind the walls is overwhelming. Very few people have any idea how many prisons there are, where they are, how many people are in them or what it is like inside. Occasionally they will read media reports of riots or escapes, on the one hand, or how apparently luxurious prison life is, on the other, but the general rule is that out of sight is out of mind.

But every now and then the lid is blown off and the reality exposed; the public is suddenly and graphically shown what *really* goes on. The 1990 revolt at Strangeways prison did this in a spectacular fashion and, although the press was virulently condemnatory of the actual rioters, much of the true barbarity of British gaols *was* exposed. Suddenly, the whole country was forced to acknowledge that 'civilised' and 'democratic' Britain consistently locks up more people and for longer terms than any other European country, including Turkey. Many people learned for the first time that in local gaols[1] such as Strangeways, men were being held three to a cell for 22 hours a day with no sanitation, one shower per week and one change of underwear. And those who watched the TV news coverage saw for themselves prison officers beating on their shields and shouting threats to 'get' the prisoners when they came off the roof.

The uprising that began at Strangeways in Manchester on 1 April 1990 became the longest protest in the history of the British prison system and sparked a wave of revolt in over 20 gaols. Before the dust had begun to settle, politicians were hastily remembering the words of the notice outside the gaols and rushing to restore a modicum of credibility and prevent such resistance in future. They did this on two completely different levels simultaneously and did their utmost to ensure the two remained separate. Firstly, amid massive publicity and in order to pacify liberal opinion and be seen to be taking action, they set up the Woolf Inquiry, the most far-reaching inquiry ever instigated into British prisons, headed by Lord Woolf, a judge with a liberal reputation. Secondly, and far more quietly and ruthlessly, they instigated a massive criminal investigation into the disturbances, pointing the finger in *this* inquiry, not at the system, but at the individuals who had dared to challenge it. At a series of trials in 1992-3, 23 men were gaoled for a total of over 140 years for offences such as riot and conspiracy to commit Grievous Bodily Harm. The ground was laid to deter future protests with a new law of Prison Mutiny.

By 1991, when the Woolf Report was published, prison conditions had been exposed so thoroughly that no politician or journalist dared defend them or extol the virtues of imprisonment. There was already a vocal body of liberal opinion which had been increasingly expressing its worries and fears since 1987, the year the prison population reached a then all-time high and spilled over into police cells, army camps and the horrific prison ship, the *Earl William*, which was used to house asylum-seekers until it blew off its moorings in a storm. While this body of opinion, which included reform groups and the government's own prisons inspectorate, had no interest in or

1. Prisons situated within towns, designed to serve the surrounding areas. They mainly accommodate prisoners serving relatively short sentences (under five years) and those on remand.

regard for those prisoners who had staged the Strangeways protest, they were more than keen to use the momentum created to push forward their agenda. In the two years which followed the uprising, they did this extremely successfully. There was still virtually no mention of the systematic brutality by prison officers against those they 'cared' for, or the climate of terror this engendered, but the official line did become one of concern about prison conditions. Overcrowding was to be tackled and the disgusting ritual of 'slopping out'[2] ended; there would be more exercise, more activities in gaol, more communication between the prisoner and the outside world. And there would be less use of imprisonment overall; prison clearly didn't 'work':

'Imprisonment can lessen people's sense of responsibility for their actions and reduce their self-respect... Imprisonment is costly for the individual, for the prisoner's family and for the community'. *Custody, Care and Justice. White Paper 1991. 1.16*

Even before the Woolf Report was published, Home Secretary Kenneth Baker was promising an end to slopping out by the year 2000, and a package of other improvements; after its publication, he brought the date forward to 1994 and introduced more measures to facilitate contact between prisoners and their families. As a *direct result* of the actions of those who took part in the 1990 prison uprisings, there were a whole number of small but significant improvements in day-to-day prison conditions: a substantial increase in the number of visits permitted (from monthly to weekly in most cases), the ending of routine censorship of prisoners' mail and, perhaps most importantly of all, the introduction of public telephones. All these measures were easy, in practical terms, for the Prison Service to implement (and in the case of the telephones, lucrative) but they had never been introduced before due to fierce opposition from the Prison Officers' Association (POA) and huge scares about security. The Strangeways events had changed, for a while, the balance of power.

This mood was short-lived and now, four years later, the backlash is in full swing. The drive towards reform, which the Strangeways protesters compelled the govern-

---

2. In gaols with no toilet facilities in the cells (47 per cent of prison places at the time of the revolt; 11 per cent in 1994, according to the Prison Service's *Corporate Plan 1994-97*) prisoners are provided with buckets which they use as toilets and are allowed out of their cells to empty, or 'slop out' only at certain fixed times. In 1989 the Chief Inspector of Prisons, Judge Stephen Tumim, made it clear that he condemned the practice as unhygienic and humiliating.

ment to adopt, has been submerged under a torrent of carefully manufactured counter-propaganda and it is back to business as usual. In fact, business is on the increase and the prison population is soaring. Sentence lengths are increasing and conditions in gaol are being deliberately harshened.

Britain still has the highest prison population in western Europe and, although the number of people in gaol in England and Wales fell by 5,000 in the three months following the implementation of the 1991 post-Strangeways Criminal Justice Act, it immediately began rising again and is now increasing at a staggering rate. By the end of 1993 250-500 more prisoners were being incarcerated *each week* and there were 1,000 more prisoners in the system than the official capacity allowed. By March 1994 nine local prisons were more than 40 per cent overcrowded; Leicester prison was 77 per cent overcrowded, with 344 prisoners in accommodation built for 194. Between January 1993 and March 1994 the prison population of England and Wales rose from 41,000 to 48,800 and by October 1994 it was over 50,100 and lurching towards the 1987 all-time high of 51,300. The number of women in gaol rose by a third between January 1993 and November 1994. In Scotland (which has a separately administered prison system and, relative to the population as a whole, an even higher rate of imprisonment than England and Wales) the prison population rose seven per cent between 1992 and 1993.

And those who are being sent to gaol today in ever-increasing numbers are the same kind of people who were there in 1990 and who have always been sent there:

- Young people – half those sent to prison are under 25;
- Black people – 16 per cent of male and 26 per cent of female prisoners are black or from other ethnic groups (compared to 5.5 per cent of the overall population of Britain) and there are over 600 asylum-seekers and refugees in detention, whose only crime was to flee their own country;
- Poor people – in 1993 22,754 men and women were gaoled in England and Wales because they were unable to pay fines and civil debts (504 of them were Poll Tax non-payers).

Forty three per cent of prisoners have no educational qualifications and an estimated 50 per cent have problems with basic functional literacy. Thirty eight per cent of young offenders have already been in council care. In 1991 (when the overall prison population was a lot lower than it is today) the Institute of Psychiatry estimated there were 1,100 prisoners in need of immediate psychiatric care and a further 16,000 suffering from other mental health problems. There were 221 suicides and over 3,000 reported incidents of self-harm in gaols in England and Wales during the four years up to September 1994.

So the poor, the working class and the vulnerable go to gaol, while rich criminals who steal millions, take enormous bribes and live in luxury off the backs of the working class are very occasionally scapegoated by their peers and sent to an open prison for a few years. But far more often they are rewarded with OBEs, knighthoods, ministers' portfolios, directorships and yet more stolen money.

The death-knell of the post-Strangeways reforms was sounded in 1993 by Home Secretary Michael Howard's call for greater austerity in prison regimes and the ridiculous assertion by Prime Minister John Major that 'prison works'. This was despite the Home Office's *own* research showing that to achieve a one per cent drop in crime merely by increased custody, it would be necessary to imprison 25 per cent more people.

Wiping out the gains of the Strangeways uprising has not proven quite as simple as the government and its friends might have wished. Even Derek Lewis, Director General of the Prison Service, recognises this. Speaking in the wake of the protest which destroyed Wymott prison in September 1993, he said:

'Now indeed we probably face a more volatile situation [than before Strangeways] because expectations among the prisoner population have been increased as a result of the Woolf Report.'

Following its almost total destruction in the 1990 protest, Strangeways prison was rebuilt, refurbished and, as part of the government's ongoing privatisation drive, was market-tested: put out to tender but with the 'in-house team' (management, supported by the POA) allowed to bid to run it. The staff won the contract and the Manchester gaol is now being extolled as a model of a new 'industrial' prison.

The prison officially reopened on 27 May 1994 and the press were invited in by Derek Lewis to wonder at the gleaming wings and workshops. But prisoners in the refurbished gaol knew who to thank for the improvements and told journalists:

'The better conditions in here are not down to the prison department. But for the riot, we would still be in the same old jail banged up all day and slopping out.'

'The rioters brought this about. These conditions . . . should not have cost the lives of a prisoner, a prison officer and two huge court trials. They should have done it years ago but it took a riot to get them to do it.' (*Manchester Evening News*)

This book is written in tribute to the 1990 prison protesters; it is the story of the men who brought the sewer that was then Strangeways to public attention.

Nicki Jameson and Eric Allison

Strangeway prison: one of Europe's largest gaols

Part One

The Strangeways uprising

Chapter One

The alarm sounds

It went off in the chapel on the morning of April Fools' Day 1990. It was no joke though. There were serious grievances at Strangeways. At the time, however, most prisoners, if they thought about it at all, thought they would be in the chapel for 24 hours, attract some attention, maybe win on a few of the points, undoubtedly lose a little remission. Nobody had any idea of the scale of the events which would unfold.

The Church of England chaplain, Noel Proctor, rose to thank the visiting Church Army preacher for his sermon. What happened next was tape-recorded along with the sermon. Proctor was apparently recording the service for distribution to a prayer group. The recipients of the transcript became, however, the Woolf Inquiry, Manchester Crown Court and the press.

Noel Proctor: After that remarkable message that has . . .

A prisoner [*later identified as Paul Taylor*]: I would like to say, right, that this man has just talked about blessing of the heart and a hardened heart can be delivered. No it cannot, not with resentment, anger and bitterness and hatred being instilled in people.

[*General noise, over which*]:

A prisoner: Fuck your system, fuck your rules.

[*Applause*]

Proctor: Right lads, sit down.

[*More noise*]

Proctor: Right lads, down. Down. Come on, this is no way to carry on in God's house.

[*More noise*]

A prisoner: Fuck your system.

[*More noise*]

Proctor: Right lads, sit down. This is completely out of order. Sit down.

A prisoner: Why is it? It's been waiting to happen for ever. It will never change.

Proctor: Come on. This is terrible.

[*More noise; banging, shouting, cheering*]

All of you who want to go back to your cells go to the back of the church please.

A prisoner: What? You're a fucking hypocrite, you.

Proctor: I'm trying to help you, to keep you.

A Prisoner: Leave it, mate.

[*More noise until microphone goes dead*]

Paul Taylor describes the pictures that accompanied this soundtrack from the moment his speech was interrupted:

'Prison officers came towards me; Prison Chaplain Noel Proctor was pulling the lead of the microphone. Later he explained to me that when he pulled it, it had struck him in the eye. The Prison Service attempted to sway public opinion by releasing that the chaplain had been assaulted.

'Thereafter a situation developed in a matter of seconds, and prisoners began expressing the feelings inside their hearts. I myself ran to the back of the chapel and began ushering prison officers out of the chapel to a place of safety. . . I also escorted Mr Proctor through the vestry of the chapel to a place of safety. He can confirm this.

'Keys which had been taken from a prison officer were passed to me. The doors at the back of the chapel leading into the chapel from the central rotunda were then opened and I shouted: "It is time everyone had a little association and communication." I then proceeded to unlock all of those prisoners not already unlocked, throughout the prison, to free them from the restraints of being locked in a prison cell without sanitation or washing facilities.'[1]

---

1. *Fight Racism! Fight Imperialism!* 96 August/September 1990.

Mayhem[2]

The media coverage in the days to come would allege that at this point the chief aims of the prisoners who ran to other parts of the gaol were to attack and even kill those men in gaol for sexual offences, the so-called 'nonces', segregated under Rule 43(a) [3], and to consume enormous quantities of drugs. It is certainly true that drugs were taken, particularly the tranquilliser Temazepam, and several prisoners were evacuated from the gaol and taken to hospital suffering from overdoses. There is also no doubt that alleged sex-offenders were beaten up, as were prisoners who had been informers either in or outside prison and a former police officer. There has, however, never been any evidence to support the contention that these acts were orchestrated by those who were later to emerge as leading figures in the protest, nor any to back up the stories of kangaroo courts, castrations and other excesses.

'How did they lose it?'

The questions that initially concerned the press, Parliament and the Woolf Inquiry after the uprising were not to do with the role of the prisoners in the chapel – they were assumed to be potentially violent and dangerous if given the opportunity – but of prison officers. How were the prisoners given that opportunity? How many officers were in the chapel? How did they lose control? Were they understaffed, overwhelmed or did they just run away? These and related questions were asked and answered in a hundred different ways by the Prison Officers Association (POA), Prison Governors' Association (PGA), Home Office and media. Here is what Paul Taylor had to say on the subject:

2   This was the front-page headline in the *Manchester Evening News* third and fourth editions on 2 April. The first and second read '20 Dead' and '20 Dead?'
3.   Under Prison Rule 43 prisoners are kept in segregation, away from 'normal location', separated from other prisoners. There are two distinct parts to the rule, dealing with two separate categories of prisoner:
    43(b) segregates 'subversive' prisoners in the interests of 'Good Order And Discipline (GOAD)' and
    43(a) segregates those prisoners who choose to be isolated for their own protection, those who fear attack from other prisoners.
The majority of prisoners on 43(a) have committed or been charged with sexual offences, especially against children, but other prisoners who choose to be 'on the Rule' include informers and ex-policemen or prison officers.

'Within the chapel there were approximately 15 prison officers and . . . many more immediately outside the chapel; so for the Prison Service to suggest there were only "half a dozen prison officers present" is simply an attempt to distance themselves further from the very fact that everyone would stand in judgement of their lack of commitment to contain the situation and to further their call for recruitment of more uniformed prison officers.'

In fact the official spokesmen of the Prison Service, as opposed to the 'unofficial voice' of the POA, agree with Paul Taylor:

'Last Sunday a warning had been received that an incident would be initiated in the chapel. That warning *was* acted upon. Additional staff were allocated to escort prisoners to the chapel and there was an increased staff presence during the service. As an additional precautionary measure all Rule 43 prisoners were excluded on Sunday from attending the service. The normal complement of prisoners at the chapel varies between 200 and 400. On Sunday approximately 300 prisoners attended the service.' *Home Office statement to press, 5 April 1990*

From the chapel to the roof

Although protesters who were in the know beforehand had only anticipated a limited action in the chapel itself, once the prison staff had fled it soon became apparent that bigger things were possible. Among the first prisoners to leave the chapel and go onto the roof was Alan Lord. He describes his progress to the roof:

'On reaching the back of the church . . . I exited with other inmates, Paul Taylor being somewhere within them and . . . I was even more taken aback to find no confrontation by any warders; the place seemed completely deserted . . . After going three-quarters of the way round the rotunda, my attention was automatically drawn to the scaffolding and I felt this compulsion to enter and climb it to the roof. So on quickly gazing through the meshing which covers the rotunda, I noticed to my delight that some had already made an opening near the church. I joined the few people going through.
    'After entering through the mesh I quickly scaled the scaffolding. This extra physical activity was most exhilarating and the prospect of reaching the top was

thrilling because I was about to observe the living outside world for the first time in ten years of incarceration. Every other institution I'd been in, the structure is designed so you can only look at concrete walls and they are only two storeys high.

'I noticed a large number of men occupying F wing roof and obviously in some confrontation with warders below...I noticed that A wing roof was unoccupied so, with caution at first, I crossed from F wing to A wing...On finally reaching this roof I admittedly began to vent my ten years of frustration and anger over my illegal treatment and that of many other lifers who I know who've been subjected to the same brutal force by the warders, both mentally and physically, not just in Strangeways but many other institutions around the British Isles...So this relative freedom naturally brought a reaction and I began to disassemble the roof with complete joy and frustration...

'During this process I somewhat stupidly, put my right hand through the skylight window and received severe lacerations to my hand and my forearm. Both were profusely bleeding. I did take regard of these cuts but determination to view the world was my objective and, therefore, I proceeded in a more reasonable manner, but admit to dislodging a few slates. Yes, even though I was angry I was consciously aware of my actions and therefore took the precaution of throwing them within an empty vicinity. Certainly taking considerable care over directly physically assaulting any warders. Obviously I was aware of the nature of a foolish act and the serious consequences it could cause. At no time did I deliberately vent my emotional anger on warders even though some had gathered at the farthest side of the prison interior car park, which was situated near the end of A wing. Admittedly, many insulting words were passed between us and these warders and some of their actions were quite provocative and they made quite obvious the serious consequences, once this siege was over: the penalty on coming down would be broken limbs...My reaction was rebuke and laughter at such pathetic creatures now that the usual bosses' role was reversed and it wasn't an inmate on the end of their batons, fists and boots in some segregation unit.'

The remand wing

Using the bunch of keys taken from the prison officer in the chapel, a small group of prisoners ran around the gaol, unlocking the cells. Others opened cells with less conventional tools, such as iron bars and fire extinguishers. Remand prisoners describe how the protest arrived on their wing:

'When I looked out of the spy hole in the door I saw lads running all over the place. Some had masks on and others were wearing prison officers' uniforms...Cell doors were being booted in and then after a while our cell door was knocked off its hinges. There was a lad...at the door. He had a piece of cloth with eye holes cut over his head. He was holding one of the bars that holds weights and he must have used that to force open the door.' *Mark Lloyd (statement to police)*

'About 12.45 to 1300 hours I heard the sound of breaking glass on the wings and we knew then there was definitely trouble and a few minutes later our cell door was unlocked. The prisoner that unlocked us was wearing a pullover sleeve over his head with eye holes in it. He said, "Everybody out".' *Gordon Lipscombe (statement to police)*

'When it spread to remands it was around 12, 12.30, 12.45...about then and when my door got opened I knew by then of course what had taken place in the chapel...Soon after I got unlocked from my cell on day one the remand wing went up...set alight...the halls on remand filled with thick black smoke...a cry of "Everyone to the main prison!" went up and loads of us went onto the main prison...

'Some kids I know went back to sleep on remand and left the gaol when the MUFTI[4] came in and retook remands on Monday morning. I stayed on the

4. MUFTI = Minimum Use of Force Tactical Intervention.
The prison version of the riot police. Formed and trained in secret and first used at Gartree in 1978, the existence of the MUFTI squads was only publicly admitted after their use at Wormwood Scrubs in 1979 to disperse a non-violent demonstration by prisoners, using Maximum Force:
'Prisoners from C wing saw about 300 prison warders form up in the exercise yard. They were wearing helmets, padded jackets, gloves and carrying four foot long wooden staves and riot shields...At about 10pm the cells on the landing were closed, locking out the peaceful protesters. Then, as one prisoner put it, "the riot squad went mad". The rioting warders burst into the wing and began assaulting everyone in sight...including a disabled prisoner who was beaten to the floor and then beaten while he was on the floor. If it had not been for the fact that some warders, not involved in the riot, opened some cells for refuge, injuries would have been even more serious and widespread. The rioting warders also entered the cells and smashed the prisoners' personal possessions. Before the prisoners were allowed back into the cells, they were forced to run the gauntlet of the riot-squad – staves, boots and fists were used.' *Hands Off Ireland! November 1979.*
In 1989 the MUFTI squads were officially replaced with 'Control and Restraint (C&R) teams' (see Appendix) and it was actually these that were in operation during the Strangeways siege. From the prisoners' point of view, however, there was not a lot of difference.

Damage to B Wing resulting from the uprising

convicted side on Sunday night because it was a sight to behold, a real novelty to sit on the roof with around 200 to 350 people at midnight. All I could think was "I wonder which section of Rule 47 Para 6 this comes under…" ' *David Bowen*

Reaction to this new-found liberation varied tremendously. As David Bowen describes, some prisoners hardly ventured out of their cells or did so only in order to find the best way out of the gaol and back into the custody of the waiting officers. Some were terrified; some, like David, simply watched enthralled as their 'home' was destroyed around them; others joined in with gusto.

Not a screw in sight

The *Manchester Evening News* of Monday 2 April carried a 'diary' of events which began with the blatant lie, 'By noon hundreds of prisoners were fighting running battles with staff through corridors, workrooms and yards.' The truth was that by noon prison officers had abandoned not just the chapel but the entire gaol. The 'vulnerable prisoners', for whom POA officials would later shed crocodile tears by the bucket, were hastily and unceremoniously abandoned to their fate. POA Vice Chair George Eliot spoke to the press outside the prison gates of the 'unbelievable…bravery and gallantry of the staff of all ranks' and the 'horrific' scenes inside the gaol. When directly asked how many members of staff were actually inside the prison, he was forced to admit that the answer was none, although there were plenty 'on the perimeter'.

The *Manchester Evening News* 'diary' continues:

'More fires were breaking out all over the prison. Flames from a blaze in the prison gym leapt 20 feet into the air.[5] Outnumbered and taking casualties, the warders beat a retreat to secure the prison perimeters. By 1pm scores of prisoners were on

---

5. When interviewed by police Alan Lord was asked if he set the gym alight. He replied that in the time he had been at Strangeways he had never once received a recreation period and did not even know the building in question was a gymnasium.

the roofs of the blocks that radiate like the spokes of a wheel from the centre. Many wore masks to hide their identity. Some wore captured prison officers' uniforms and wielded weapons.'

Of nearly 1,650 prisoners in the gaol, up to 1,100 were involved on that first day. In the course of the day 700 of those were to surrender and be transferred, along with 400 of the non-participants.

The prisoners who stayed in the liberated gaol after the initial frenzy was over began to organise themselves: exchanging torn clothing for garments in better repair and constructing barricades from cell furniture and places to sleep for the night.

For one-time Strangeways prisoner, Eric Allison, on the other side of Manchester, 1 April 1990 started off as an ordinary day:

'It couldn't have been more ordinary in fact; not an inkling of the momentous event to come, nor how that event would dominate my life for years to come; cooking and eating breakfast with my kids, then driving over to north Manchester to see my mam and dad. A very ordinary Sunday.

'Then things altered. As I returned from my parents' home, I pulled up outside our house and my lad came rushing out to greet me. He shouted, "Dad, it's gone bang off at Strangeways. There's hundreds of cons on the roof!" For a second I thought he might be trying to April Fool me, but he knew my views on Strangeways and I knew he wouldn't kid about such things. He said he'd heard the news on the local radio. We decided to drive down there right away.

'Looking down on the gaol as we approached, it was a sight I'd seen many, many times and which in the past had never failed to depress me. I knew the pain and misery those wretched walls contained. But this time was different: my heart sang with joy and my eyes filled with tears. We pulled over and I let the vision engulf me ...

'It is hard to estimate how many lads were on the roof – certainly a hundred, possibly two. Equally hard to describe what they were doing but I could feel the exultation that they were feeling, the sense of defiance and pride.

'We parked the car and tried to walk to the main entrance of the nick in Southall Street but the police, who were already there in huge numbers, stopped our progress.

'There must have been a couple of hundred people there. Many clearly had a vested interest; their tattoos told the tale, as did the gleeful expressions on their faces. There were handshakes, backslapping — reminiscent of Wembley when the goal goes in — utterances of amazement and incredulity: "Look at them, just look at those lads up there." "Can you believe it? Jesus Christ, can you *believe* it?"

'The press were also now arriving in numbers. They had not yet been briefed and were running around trying to gather information: "Who are you? Have you been in there? What's that wing? How would they have got on the roof? What's it like in there? *Why are they doing this?*"

'Police were arriving by the coachload (plenty of overtime there) and were extending their cordon around the gaol and trying to marshal the ever-increasing number of spectators. There were several fire engines and ambulances.

'For the next couple of hours we wandered around the streets surrounding the prison. The streets of Strangeways are mean streets, filled with mean-looking factories and warehouses and in the very centre of them — with its giant, domineering chimney — was the meanest of the lot. Strangeways prison was both warehouse and factory, storing only humans and producing only hate. And there we were, watching its take-over by the, mainly young, lions of men on the roof.

'We left, reluctantly, around 5pm. That evening I spoke to an old pal from London, a man in his mid-60s, fit, hard, not usually given to showing emotion. His voice that night was full of passion. He was an expert on Strangeways; he'd been taken there after the Hull riot of '76. The van took him straight to the block, by-passing the prison reception. By this he knew the sort of reception he was going to get. Even so, he was surprised at the ferocity and the obvious planning of it all. The prisoners, three of them, still with their hands cuffed behind their backs, were made to walk along a passage, the walls of which were lined by screws holding truncheons and wearing pillow-cases over their heads. They were beaten and kicked black and blue. Now he spoke in almost loving terms of the lads who had captured the stinking place.

'As I lay in bed, my head and my heart were with the lads on the roof of Her Majesty's Prison Manchester. Only tonight, it wasn't Her Majesty's; it was theirs.'

Operation Rescue – the police's flying eye

As soon as the police were notified of the uprising, they responded with the inappropriately named, from anybody's point of view, Operation Rescue, which included the immediate dispatch of a £1 million 'eye in the sky' helicopter. The main aim of this was to 'identify the ringleaders' ready for future prosecution. The inaccuracy of this so-called high-tech identification is notorious as the pictures are fuzzy, indistinct and often those identified could be anyone. Ironically, though, Alan Lord would later use the helicopter video film in court to prove that he was on the roof rather than on E wing at the point Derek White and other alleged sex-offenders were being beaten.

The roof photographed from the helicopter

Home Office statements

The Home Office Public Relations Department issued its first statement at 3.40pm: 'At 11am a disturbance started in the chapel at Strangeways Prison when some 300 prisoners attacked staff. Those prisoners then gained access to the chapel roof and then broke into the living accommodation in the main prison. Other prisoners, including those on remand, joined in the disturbance and staff had to be withdrawn. The perimeter is secure.'

At 5pm it added: 'Approximately 500 inmates have now surrendered and arrangements are being made to disperse them to other establishments. Meanwhile, damage is continuing. There are no known escapes. We have no information on casualties or the extent of damage.'

And at 9.35pm: 'Between 8.30 and 9pm prison staff regained control of the one wing. No seriously injured inmates were found on that wing. Fires are not under control. Prisoners continue to give themselves up. At the moment there are still about 700 loose.'

Night time

Night fell. The men inside the liberated Strangeways chatted far into the night, high on a strange sense of freedom. Alan Lord:

'During that late evening I settled down, the occurrences of the day obliterated from my mind. I suffer from insomnia, brought about by the prison staff's voices at night time, by the warders on duty wearing heavy studded boots and laughing and rattling the keys when turning the night clock on and . . . inmates' late night activity of playing radios and record players and occasionally talking until the early hours of the morning out of the windows. So every time I awoke, people were still either engaged in conversation or walking about . . . taking the opportunity to enjoy each other's company.'

Some prisoners stayed on the roof until 4am that first night, watching the world below. David Bowen was one of them. Earlier in the evening he had listened to the Top Twenty on Radio One 'blaring through a loud speaker that had come from the chapel and was rigged up to a radio and tape. It was getting dark; around 250 people seemed to be on the roof. People were looking out over Manchester. It was a really nice sight. I sat and looked at what seemed thousands of people at the end of the road. Ice cream, hot dog, all kinds of stands started to pop up; cameras everywhere, hundreds of them watching us, watching them, watching us. Still I didn't seem to realise what I was in the middle of. It took a couple of years to fully understand the enormous situation I was in . . .'

Chapter Two

Mounting tension

It had been boiling up for weeks, months, years even. When Chaplain Noel Proctor gave evidence to the Woolf Inquiry that in the weeks before the uprising there were 'no complaints' from prisoners in the block, he must have been lying or stone deaf. The complaints were as continuous as the oppression.

There is incontrovertible evidence that the prison staff knew there would be some form of protest on the Sunday but they made no serious attempt to prevent it. A riot suited their campaign to prove they were understaffed.

Barry and Tony's protest

A week before the revolt, on Monday 26 March 1990, Barry Morton was pulled aside for a strip-search after a visit. Prison officers maintained that his mother, who had been ill and was visiting for the first time in ten months, had brought him drugs. A large number of screws violently grabbed him, carried him down to D1, the punishment block, where he was beaten up, sustaining a black eye and a swollen nose. The following day, the 27th, he and Tony Bush, who had also been in the block, were allowed back on to C wing, from where they climbed onto the roof and stayed until the following day. Twenty prisoners originally agreed to be involved in this protest but only two went ahead with it.

Like many of the young men who found themselves in Strangeways on 1 April 1990, Barry Morton comes from the Ordsall Estate in Salford. He was 21 at the time of the revolt and was serving one sentence in Strangeways while awaiting trial for another matter. He describes the 27-28 March protest as follows:

'We waited for the last slop-out when they give out the supper and blagged special sick;[1] then we ran down the landing, one on each side, jumped, (well, climbed!) over the locked gates and into a hole which we had done during the day, pulled it open and got onto the scaffold and, bingo, onto the roof.

'To be truthful, it was terrifying up there. There we were, 50 to 70 feet from the ground, doing bunny hops just to keep our balance because the slates were wet. It was raining and they were very slippery. So at night time, when we knew we were staying up, we removed enough slates so we could relax and have a good grip and enjoyed the sight of Manchester. When morning came we called it a day.'

After their protest, Barry and Tony were quite surprised not to be beaten up again; instead they were fed and left to sleep until the following day when they saw the governor who said the matter was being adjourned for the police to consider.

Paul Taylor

Paul Taylor was already in the block, charged with assaulting a notorious prison officer named Duffy. He talked to other prisoners about the constant oppression and what to do about it. Together a few of them agreed it would be a good idea to stage a 'sit-in protest'. Rumours that such an event was to take place had already been circulating and they decided that they would make the rumours come true. They then talked to other prisoners in the punishment wing who agreed that: 'certainly something should be done in respect of bringing the governor to realise that there were real tensions that could not possibly be ignored any further as they had been on so many occasions in the past.'[2]

The 'liquid cosh'

On Saturday 31 March there was a limited protest in the chapel. After a film show, the back two rows (the 'staunch' ones) refused to move for half an hour. Paul Taylor made a speech. Principal Officer Pete Hancox (whom we will hear much from later in his capacity as a POA spokesman) promised to listen to their grievances and make

---

1. Prisoners are expected to 'report sick' at specified times; in emergencies they have to put themselves on 'special sick'.
2. Unpublished extract from letter sent to *Fight Racism! Fight Imperialism!* 23 May 1990.

improvements, so they returned to their cells. That evening a black prisoner, Andrew Kazim, was beaten in the corridor in full view of other prisoners and injected with the 'liquid cosh'[3]. The prisoners were sickened by this and decided to go ahead with a protest in the chapel the following day.

Barry Morton describes the 'liquid cosh':

'It is a powerful drug that can ruin any human being for the rest of their life. The effects are as follows: it slows you down and makes your mind hallucinate and makes you lose your memory and slows down your speech. When you don't know you are doing it, you talk to yourself, but you find it hard to hold conversations with anybody for a long period. You don't remember doing things. Sometimes you live like this for days or maybe weeks, even months, depending on how much they inject you with.

'Seven prison officers held Andrew Kazim down and injected him several times and turned him into a cabbage. It's a brown thick liquid that affects you the minute it's injected into the body.'

Domenyk Noonan and the PLA

A fortnight before Strangeways went up, a Category B prisoner was moved from Strangeways to Hull prison in a Category A van[4]. They took him off the exercise yard and transferred him with sirens blaring and a helicopter overhead. His name was Domenyk Noonan and he came from a large and locally well-known family in Cheetham Hill, Manchester.

In 1989 Domenyk launched the Prisoners' League Association (PLA), which had

3. Largactyl, known in prison as the 'liquid cosh', is the most commonly administered of a range of psychotropic drugs used extensively for control rather than medicinal purposes. For a detailed exposé of the use of drugs for control purposes see: *Medical Power in Prisons* by Joe Sim, Open University Press 1990 and *The Liquid Cosh* by Mickey Peterson, Breakout Collective 1984.
4. The 'security categories' currently in use were introduced in 1968, at the same time as the 'dispersal' system of high security prisons. Prisoners are categorised on reception as A, B, C or D, according to the perceived risk to the community should they escape. A and many B Cats are housed in the dispersal prisons, the remainder of the Bs and Cs in local and 'training' prisons, Ds in open establishments. The idea was not just to 'make the punishment fit the crime' but that as a prisoner became rehabilitated he would be progressively decategorised. In practice, this mechanism immediately became part of the 'carrot and stick' apparatus, a prisoner's eventual category being dependent far more on conformity to the prison system than on any notion of rehabilitation.

previously existed in a very different form entitled the Prisoners' Liberation Army. The PLA was to be an organisation of prisoners and of their supporters. Its aims were:

1. Initiating litigation against governors and prison staff for mistreatment of prisoners;
2. Picketing outside prisons where mistreatment is rife;
3. Arranging cheap or free transport for prisoners' visitors, and, where necessary, overnight accommodation;
4. Providing radios and other items for prisoners who cannot afford them;
5. Publishing a newsletter.

This statement of aims was published in October 1989 and the PLA planned to be fully active by January 1990. By the time Domenyk was ghosted from Strangeways in March it had not managed to implement all of its planned programme but was operating from a Manchester address and gathering support. Inside, Domenyk, calling himself 'Chief of the PLA', was recruiting prisoners to the cause. The PLA became a brotherhood in struggle. Membership was hard to define but essentially anyone who was fighting the system and wanted to be involved could count themselves as a member. They began to sign PLA at the bottom of their letters and graffiti it in cells. The hardcore membership, who were close to Domenyk, carried out some creative actions including one where a prisoner and his girlfriend superglued themselves to one another in a prison visiting room.

Although before April 1990 the system publicly either ignored the PLA altogether or dismissed it as a piece of nonsense, in truth they feared it, especially at Strangeways, where it had the support of many young Mancunians and Liverpudlians, doing short sentences or on remand, who had spent most of their adult lives in gaol and who wanted to fight back.

After the uprising there were some attempts (in particular a *File on Four* programme broadcast on BBC Radio Four on 8 June 1990) to prove that the PLA had organised the Strangeways uprising. There was no evidence to support this theory but Domenyk's removal to Hull certainly demonstrates that the prison authorities were fully aware that Strangeways was at boiling point and wanted to rid themselves of someone who they thought would capitalise on the situation.

The attempt to lay the blame for what followed at the door of the PLA is consistent with government propaganda following most uprisings in or out of prison. After the inner-city riots of 1981 and 1985, after the anti-Poll Tax riot on 31 March 1990, after many such occasions when large numbers of people have fought back against their oppression, the emphasis is always on a 'small group of violent and fanatical trouble-makers' who must be denounced by all reasonable people, including those who 'genuinely' want to protest about prison conditions, racism, the Poll Tax etc. These 'agitators' are not really concerned with the issues in question; they have a hidden and threatening agenda.

Of course it is a lot harder to make this story convincing in a prison situation where the 'violent fanatics' cannot be portrayed as 'outsiders'. But the basic aim is the same: to pick off and isolate the most determined so that the majority who have risen up in anger will either be turned against the few or simply terrorised out of future activity for fear they will become targets themselves. Naming the PLA as the instigators was one attempt at achieving this end; it was sensational but unsuccessful as it was too far from the truth to be believed in any quarter. The murder charges which were brought against six men and the long sentences handed down for riot and conspiracy did the job more effectively.

'Hate and intimidation'

John McGranaghan was moved out of Strangeways a few days after Domenyk. He says of Domenyk: 'They wanted to give him a hard time because he would educate prisoners in the sense he'd make them aware of their rights.'

John was serving life for a series of rapes he did not commit and was released on appeal in October 1991 after ten years' false imprisonment. During his sentence he protested continually about his own case and on behalf of other prisoners. Consequently, he saw the inside of many a segregation unit:

'I arrived at Manchester in January 1990 on a lay-down[5] from the Hull Special Unit.

---

5. Measure whereby 'disruptive' prisoners are transferred to another gaol for a 'cooling-off' period of 28 days. As well as the power to punish prisoners for a variety of offences against prison rules, governors have at their disposal a range of what are often referred to as 'informal' or 'administrative' punishments; the most notorious of these is the 'lay-down', sometimes still referred to by the number CI 10/74 of the Circular Instruction under which it was first created in 1974. The original 10/74 decreed that Manchester prison should keep two secure cells permanently available to receive prisoners from Hull and Wakefield dispersal prisons. Successive lay-downs are known as the 'ghost train' and are a tried and tested method of disorientation. A detailed examination of 'informal punishment' can be found in *One-off* by Andrzy Jakubczyk and Paul Ross.

When I arrived there I could feel the atmosphere – very, very tense. One officer and a governor came to see me and said "Look, we don't want trouble here. We've got a bit of trouble, so keep it cool." And I could see for myself. When you were out of your cell they were eight or ten-handed, arms crossed, sometimes drunk – intimidation, pure intimidation. Other prisoners had been dragged off the wing and beaten up. One was Tony Bush; he came down and he had received a beating. The whole atmosphere was hate and intimidation.

'On numerous occasions I heard other prisoners asking to see governors and other individuals but I don't think any of them saw them. I wasn't even aware that O'Friel was the governor there because I never saw him; he was never, ever in the block.

'I saw the chaplain and, to be honest, I didn't like the man. When he came in to see me, he said, "Are you all right?" and I said, "Yes" and he said, "This is a good prison, good officers, nobody touches you here." I said, "That's not what I've heard". He said, "No, no, take it from me. Nobody touches you. I've been here for so many years." His whole attitude was one of *them*, one hundred per cent. When I said to him that some prisoners were being beaten up and that I'd heard it myself, he said, "No, no, some do get a bit rough and they've got to hold them down. There's nobody getting beaten up."

'Before I was sent to Gartree there were rumours all round that it was going to go off and my feeling is that prison officers wanted it to go off to help their case for better wages and more hours, but I don't think they thought that quite so much hatred was involved. I think they thought it would be a little thing and they could contain it.'

The Category A unit

The ground floor, or 'ones'[6] of D wing, Strangeways, was split in the middle: on one side 20 punishment cells which constituted the 'block'; on the other 15 cells for Category A prisoners. To one side, down a special corridor, were the two special punishment or 'silent cells'. John McGranaghan was in the Category A cells:

---

6. In Strangeways, as in most prisons built in the same period, there are four levels on each wing. Prisoners and prison staff generally refer to these as the 'ones', 'twos', 'threes' and 'fours'.

'You could walk through from the Cat A Unit to the block but if somebody was beaten in the block, you couldn't get through; you'd get five or six prison officers blocking it off.

'The Cat A regime was very bad. Even on exercise you never saw daylight. Our cells faced north west so we never saw the sun and when we went out on exercise we never saw the sky either because the exercise yard had covers over it.

'Some Cat As were on lay-down, some on remand and they were mixed together. As soon as I got there, some of them warned me that they use the MUFTI and they steam in. The atmosphere was hate and fear. A lot of people were frightened. They wanted you to walk all the way round when you went from your cell to get food, instead of walking over, to belittle you. I could understand if 100, or even 30 prisoners were all bumping into one another. My cell was right opposite the servery and they wanted me to walk all the way round, say 30 yards, when it was five yards opposite me. I refused to do it. I told other lads and they refused too so it was knocked on the head, but someone told me that the day after I left they tightened it up again.

'The conditions were scandalous. There was no light. You had to use artificial light all the time. Dirty as well. Where I was there was other people's shit on the walls.'

When asked what he thought sparked the 1990 uprising, John replied:

'Conditions, brutality, people's dignity, just "I've had enough." Why should anyone doing 18 months or three to four years put themselves on the line just for a laugh? Common sense tells you they were really pushed into it. It's hard to describe because it's not the brutality or the dirt, it's the atmosphere which is the worst part. It doesn't matter how tough you are if there's eight or nine of them and you know there's another 50 behind to come down and help them out.'

Out of the doldrums

Just one week before Strangeways went up, Her Majesty's Chief Inspector of Prisons, Judge Stephen Tumim, had published his report into Strangeways prison, based on an inspection carried out the previous July. The report is critical but generally favourable, and begins: 'Life at Manchester is a great deal nearer what it should be,

Angela Rumbold, who succeeded David Mellor as Prison Minister, and Brendan O'Friel, Governor of Strangeways

both for staff and inmates, than it was some two years ago.'

The Governor of Strangeways, Brendan O'Friel, boasted that he ran the 'fastest improving prison establishment in the country'. O'Friel, a committed Catholic and in relative terms a reformer, was appointed as governor in 1986, following upheavals which took place that year in Strangeways and many other prisons. He succeeded John Lewis, whose demise demonstrates the power of the POA at Strangeways. Lewis was forced out after a vote of no confidence by staff in his handling of the protests.

The Tumim report praised the 'developing regime' for the majority of sentenced prisoners but pointed out that remand prisoners were locked up for all but 18 hours per week. Category A prisoners were still locked up 22 hours a day and:

'rarely left their cells save for slopping out, weekly showers, collecting meals and one hour's exercise in a dirty yard... Only in-cell Education was available. When coming out of their cells which they mostly did singly or in pairs, they were made to walk around the edge of the Unit. Apart from exercise there seemed no opportunity for association. These men could expect to be located in the Unit for over a year and sometimes much longer. A video was provided once every fourteen days...' *p43, 3.24*

In the wake of the uprising, much was said about the indignities of slopping out and Kenneth Baker, who took over as Home Secretary from David Waddington six months after the Strangeways revolt, was forced to pledge to end the practice by the year 2000. The Tumim report is revealing on the moves which had already been made:

'A forward programme for the provision of integral sanitation had already started. A unit had been developed locally and the first few were being installed by a contractor. Plans existed for the local Works Department to install the rest *using inmate labour*.' *p17, 2.14 [emphasis added]*

In contrast:

> 'Work on upgrading staff toilets on the wing had been completed to a very high standard.' *p20, 2.25*

On the subject of clothing:

> 'Inmates told us that for several months they had not had full kits, being forced to wash their own shirts and socks. No proper washing facilities existed in the wings. More seriously, it emerged that there was an ongoing shortage of underpants.'

Staff told Tumim that a body-belt was used on only one occasion between June 1988 and May 1989 and that the 'special cells' were used on 64 occasions.

The conclusion to Tumim's report has an optimism that in retrospect is supremely ironic: 'There was a feeling in Manchester that in the last three years the prison had emerged from the doldrums.'

Chapter Three

On the roof

When the sun rose over Strangeways on the morning of Monday 2 April 1990, about 140 prisoners were in control of five wings of the prison. Some of those on the roof gave clenched fist salutes to the crowd below. Some wore prison officers' caps and jackets; others sported head or face coverings improvised from towels or blankets. A few strummed guitars and makeshift drums. The morning papers, without exception, reported between 11 and 20 prisoners dead, kangaroo courts, castrations and hangings. Tabloids and 'quality papers' alike were high on a weekend of 'anti-authority violence'. On Saturday the massive anti-Poll Tax demonstration through central London had been violently attacked by the police but protesters had fought back, stoned the police, looted shops in Covent Garden and Oxford Street and set fire to buildings, including the South African Embassy.

Home Secretary David Waddington told the House of Commons on the Monday afternoon: 'The general picture is of prisoners indulging in violence on other prisoners, the full consequences of which remain to be discovered.' And David Mellor, the Home Office Minister for Prisons, confirmed the government was carrying out a programme to build 24 new prisons with 10,000 places.

Waking up to 'freedom'

'After finishing my late breakfast with corn flakes and hot milk too, I climbed the roof and ventured out. Oh, what a beautiful sight to behold! A few associates were congregating and we exchanged a few pleasantries...I observed the symbol of hatred which now stood forlorn and somewhat in ruin and then I noticed the national media were situated across Southall Street within a warehouse; some inmates were conversing but the prison establishment and the police obviously considered revelations of prison brutality a serious threat to their credibility, therefore they quite deliberately opted to use the helicopter to circulate around the roofs and play the siren out loud . . . This only infuriated the people on the roof with genuine cause and it certainly amused the warders down below who were conveniently concealed by the wall.' *Alan Lord*

No dead

The prisoners inside Strangeways were shocked by the angle the media chose. Mark Williams explains:

'We all thought this was more lies told by the screws in a bid to end our protest. But just to make sure, we searched every room and every cell, every attic space, we even searched the sewers – but just like our banner said, *No dead*.'[1]

The Home Office issued a statement at 11.45am:

'Shortly after 10am this morning prison staff regained control of the four wings of the remand section [G, H, I, K.]. No resistance was encountered and six inmates surrendered peaceably. There was no evidence of any fatalities.

'No bodies were found in the remand prison. About 120 inmates are currently unaccounted for inside the prison. A total of 12 officers and 37 inmates have received treatment in outside hospitals.'

The Prison Service press department suggested to Governor O'Friel that he personally give a statement to the media at 6pm. He declined but the following was issued on his behalf:

'The governor and his staff are continuing to work towards a peaceful resolution of the situation. At 3.30pm, in a successful operation, prison staff entered the kitchen area to retrieve stores. This exercise was carried out in order to regain control of food and equipment which had been left in the kitchen. Further prisoners have sur-

1. *Fight Racism! Fight Imperialism!* 96 August/September 1990.

rendered and there are currently 114 inmates at large within the prison.'

The following day, many papers carried pictures of the 'No dead' banner. Alongside articles which still insisted on a death toll of 20 (except for *The Sun* which put it up to 30). Both *The Daily Telegraph* and *The Times* of 3 April quoted Home Secretary, Waddington, describing the riot as a 'very severe setback' to 'prison reform':

'Sadly, the short-term consequences of this incident will be to worsen conditions elsewhere just when real improvements were flowing from the combined effect of our policies on criminal justice and the prison building programme.'

The prisoners responded to all this with another banner: *Media contact now*.

'Fears and tears'

A phone-call made from inside Strangeways to the *Manchester Evening News* listed prisoners' demands as follows: better visiting facilities, including the permitting of physical contact with visitors and a play area for children, especially for remand prisoners whose families could at that time generally expect to wait two hours for a 15-minute visit during which no physical contact was allowed; Category A prisoners to be allowed to wear their own clothes and be sent food parcels; longer exercise periods and an end to 23-hour a day lock-up.

Michael Unger of the *Manchester Evening News* was allowed into the gaol at 11.10am on 3 April as an 'independent observer'. His reporters on the scene had phoned him when the *Media contact* banner was unfurled and he had rung the Home Office to offer his services. The Prison Service had dismissed the idea of taking the gaol back by overwhelming force the previous day, although Governor O'Friel had been on the point of authorising a full-scale attack. They now appeared eager at the possibility of negotiations. Unger met prisoners, including John Hughes and Eric Bell, who described to him their grievances about the system, as well as their fears of reprisals were they to surrender. The grievances were listed as: mental and physical brutality, misuse of drugs in controlling prisoners, poor food and cramped conditions. Unger promised to publish them in the following day's *Manchester Evening News*. He kept this promise.

Unger obviously enjoyed his day at the centre of the action as the *Manchester Evening News* 'exclusive' of 4 April shows. It is entitled 'I see fears and tears of the men in the hell-hole jail' and although the *Manchester Evening News* editor was told a few wild untruths by his prison officer escorts ('Problems in the prison started when inmates from other jails flooded in four or five months ago upsetting the fine balance of the regime,') his eye-witness account is an interesting record.

'Behind the flagpole, sheltering under the huge entrance archway, 30 prison officers in full riot gear, carrying batons and shields waited ominously. Surprisingly, I soon realised there were no police officers inside the prison. The massed forces, looking as if they had come from the set of the cult film *Clockwork Orange* were all prison officers.'

'The battle for E wing'

While Michael Unger was inside the prison, the so-called 'battle for E wing' took place. Accounts of this vary but the majority of the individual allegations made in the second of the two major trials which followed the revolt arise out of this particular incident. The defendants were convicted of conspiracy to cause Grievous Bodily Harm (GBH), following allegations by prison officers that they were assaulted through the mesh with scaffolding poles.

The Woolf Report states that 12 Control and Restraint (C&R) teams launched a deliberate attack on E wing as a diversion because prisoners in the Chapel had dug a hole in the floor through to F wing below and from there were attacking officers with scaffolding poles and 'other weapons'. The authorities were particularly anxious to hold F wing as confidential records on prisoners were held there. It is well-known (see, for example, Appendix 2 on Hull 1976) that nothing inflames a rioting prisoner quite as much as reading the derisory views which psychologists, governors and officers hold about him and his friends.

David Bowen describes the events of 3 April as a 'two-pronged attack' by C&R teams in an attempt to take the gaol: one attack was 'via the chapel, the other was via E wing – these attacks were at the same time.'

And Barry Morton tells this story of 3 April:

Prisoners on the roof: including Barry Morton (top, standing), Mark Azzopardi, Paul Taylor (centre), Glynn Williams and Andrew Nelson (bottom left)

'On the third day we were all busy talking and sorting out YPs [Young Prisoners] who were scared and wanted to leave but thought they would get done in. We got their solicitors and parents up and the ones who wanted to leave left. Because we were doing this we were told there would be no disturbance towards us that day but in the afternoon about 250-300 riot police and screws came storming into the gaol with force and were setting fire to offices on E wing to smoke it out, so we couldn't see them and where they were coming from. They were everywhere, banging on their shields, shouting...they were just getting through the main part of E wing when we started to rebuild the barricades to keep them out. Some scaff bars were thrown at them to keep them out too.

'After about an hour and a half they stopped and gave up and went away...I wouldn't call it a battle; it was something they provoked first and took us by surprise, so we were forced to respond in self-defence.'

Kevin Gee was one of the prisoners convicted of conspiracy to cause GBH on 3 April 1990. At the trial, his barrister summed up in his defence as follows:

'Firstly, there is evidence that there were up to 200 Control and Restraint officers present in E wing. Secondly, they were...kitted out in clothing and equipment which made them resemble Star Wars Storm Troopers. Thirdly, their faces almost concealed by their helmets, brandishing their staffs and shields...imagine what was in the mind of the defendant...add a further ingredient to this picture. John Frederick Wright [a prison officer] gave evidence about threats [made by prison officers against prisoners]...The prosecution cannot say when Kevin Gee began to use a scaffolding pole on the mesh of E wing; they cannot say whether he heard the threats and began using a scaffolding pole. Consider in which direction the Control and Restraint officers were going. They were going towards the rotunda in order to retake E wing. They were undoubtedly excited and filled no doubt you may think with adrenaline...'

Alan Lord saw some of what went on and later went down to negotiate with the authorities on the prisoners' behalf:

'Loud shouting could be heard across the roofs from the rotunda and this seem-ed important so I and many others sauntered over and entered the building.

A commotion was in swing from E wing and when I eventually reached it by crossing the scaffolding bars and planks I noticed people boisterously shouting: "They're in the building!"

'I just stood there watching, but my attention kept being distracted by others behind me on the scaffolding. They were just calmly eating and drinking tea and so I joined them, eating some biscuits and talking. On two or three occasions I ventured back to the mesh of E wing and . . . the second time the situation had calmed down and inmates were conversing with the warders or negotiating. Some were heated, others quite cordial . . .

'During my wandering and listening to the conversations, I overheard people calling for volunteers to come down and negotiate with them. This sounded reasonable and genuine. I was consciously aware of exposing myself to being snatched but under the circumstances someone had to begin negotiating and offering terms for a settlement . . . so I for one volunteered . . . Besides me, another inmate volunteered called John Hughes.'

Negotiations

'While walking through the MUFTI, one of them said, "You shouldn't negotiate with them. It's giving in." Obviously this individual preferred confrontation rather than compromise and I knew the majority of the warders were in support of this by the electrifying stares! We were escorted to E wing 'ones' landing and guided through the gate into the newly constructed hospital, which was their main headquarters. On reaching one of the wards we all sat around a table. John Hughes did the majority of the talking and he explained the people's grievances. The discussion proceeded for a while about the dispute and then the warders expressed concern about the young offenders staying in.

'During the ensuing days I had the opportunity to explore E wing and . . . never failed to . . . notice that in this era young offenders were still being treated with a regimental discipline by having their bed sacks folded into squares and the mattresses leaning against the wall; therefore they have to remain sat on a chair all day. No wonder they kicked off.

'Anyway the warders we were negotiating with (POA chair, Peter Hancox, Dave Rigby and C&R commander, Brian Nicholson) asked us to persuade as many of them to come out as possible; I didn't give any promises but said I would certainly discuss it with young offenders, so after talking we returned to the wing.

'... I persuaded many individuals to leave the premises, not only the young, but adults too. A lot were ignorant as to the actual grievances, therefore John Hughes and I, on three separate occasions, escorted various inmates out and right to the hospital wing and on each occasion were permitted to return.

· 'In fact... on many other occasions in the ensuing weeks I discharged and persuaded many individuals to leave and even on one occasion discharged some young offenders I caught sniffing glue in a cell. I discharged them for their own good and everyone else's.'

More tears and fears, and some snow

The state of play by the evening of day three was that the prisoners occupied most of the 'high ground' but prison officers had retaken the ground level. The Home Office issued a statement to that effect:

'During the course of the evening prison staff have had access at ground level to all wings in the main prison. No bodies have been found. Earlier today prison staff gained access to the main prison building in order to remove barricades to allow the surrender of all inmates who wished to do so. No inmates were injured during this process. Nine prison staff were taken to outside hospital for treatment. Two remain overnight for observation. Negotiations were carried out by prison staff... 31 inmates surrendered. All of those who surrendered have been interviewed, medically examined and fed. They will be transferred to other accommodation as soon as practicable.'

John Hughes himself surrendered that day, as did his co-convicted, Eric Bell. The *Daily Star* the following day picked up on their surrender, showing them coming down in tears: 'Riot jail hard nut gave in weeping'.

Michael Unger, who met and talked with both men, told the same story but with more compassion:

'Then John wept. Minutes later he gave himself up. When a tough-looking guy like that starts crying, you can't help but feel moved. Eric then told me he was going back on the roof to try to talk the others down. I walked back with him through the line of officers to make sure he wasn't snatched. Their demands included me as an independent observer, a doctor, specific deals from the solicitor and photographs of their bodies to make sure they weren't beaten up, "like they did at Risley".'

John Hughes' fears were realised; he was beaten up in the prison hospital before being transferred from Strangeways to Astley Bridge Police Station in Bolton. Like other

surrendering prisoners, he was photographed after giving himself up. He was also photographed again a few hours later at the police station. In the first picture he is unmarked; in the second he has two black eyes.

Michael Unger left the prison at 8pm. He wrote: 'During my 10 hours in the wrecked prison 31 men had given themselves up and I felt as if I had played a small part.' However, no doubt deliberately engineered by the Prison Service, the *Manchester Evening News* editor did not go back. 'Fears and tears' was the paper's best article on the prison uprising. It was the only occasion on which the men inside the occupied gaol were depicted as human beings. After that, coverage from the local daily newspaper descended to the level of the gutter and remained there for the rest of the 25 days and beyond.

John Hughes at Astley Bridge Police Station following his beating en route from Strangeways

Although on the Monday prisoners had basked in the rooftop sunshine, by Tuesday evening the weather was bitterly cold and it was starting to snow. Further snow was forecast for the following day. Rooftop banners read *E Wing held* well and *Told we will die*, a reference to the abuse and threats from prison officers on the ground and the reason a lot of prisoners who wanted to surrender didn't do so sooner.

Derek White

On 3 April Derek White, a remand prisoner who had been segregated under Rule 43(a), died at North Manchester Hospital in intensive care. He had been admitted on Sunday evening, treated for head wounds and a dislocated shoulder and was reported to be complaining of chest pains. He had been remanded in custody on 7 March at Sale Magistrates' Court on charges of indecent assault and buggery. Like the many other prisoners who have died in custody, he was a victim of a brutal and vicious system, where prison officers deliberately target weaker prisoners, leak details of their alleged offences to other men and turn a blind eye while they are beaten. Five men would later stand trial for his murder while the real culprits discussed their plans for reform.

Surrenders

Prisoners who surrendered naturally feared immediate reprisal. This facet of previous prison protests was universally well known. Indeed, at more than one of the Home Office press briefings outside the gaol, a spokesman giving assurances that transferred prisoners were being well looked after was heckled by an ex-prisoner from Hull gaol, Billy Gould, who said the Strangeways men would suffer the same fate as those from Hull in 1976.[2]

From the second day of the protest a host of different agencies were present to receive surrendering prisoners. The Home Office announced that, 'To allay prisoners' concerns the governor invited outside observers as well as the usual members of the Board of Visitors [BOV] to oversee inmate surrenders.' The police were also present and by the time of the trials which resulted from the revolt, the Home Office was referring to an 'elaborate surrender policy...formulated by Prison Service negotiators and others' at which the following were present: the Board of Visitors, each prisoner's own solicitor, independent police officers, family or friends. Prisoners we have spoken to bear this out, yet it was no insurance against retribution from prison officers and many prisoners were still beaten up, after the elaborate procedure was over and their families and solicitors had left. Some of the 'surrender' photographs tell their own stories. While the majority of prisoners are shown, a little bruised and dishevelled, standing next to grinning plain-clothes police officers, others – most notably Darren Jones and Alan Lord who, in the last days of the protest, did not voluntarily surrender but were snatched – are shown being forcibly 'restrained' by three or four riot-clad prison officers.

2. While the press were present, Billy Gould's right to free speech was respected; later on, he was arrested and charged with inciting prisoners to commit criminal acts. At his trial Alan Lord gave evidence for the defence and Gould was acquitted.

Chapter Four

'An explosion of evil'

Wednesday 4 April: The last 'mass surrender'

On the fourth day of the protest the prison Governor Brendan O'Friel spoke to the press for the first time, providing them with headline material for days to come by his emotional description of the uprising as 'an explosion of evil which was quite terrible to see'.

Twenty-nine prisoners surrendered that day; among them was David Bowen, then on remand for stealing a pair of curtains, now serving nine years for conspiracy to cause Grievous Bodily Harm, plus three years for conspiring to pervert the course of justice. He is still awaiting a further trial for escaping from custody. David was astounded that he could be convicted of conspiring to do anything:

> 'I was on remand in the prison – the riot started on the convicted side of the gaol and the two sides never meet. I found it hard to understand how the Crown could say I was involved in a conspiracy to riot when I didn't even know until my cell door was opened that any riot was to take place. But my barrister said they could say you flew around in the helicopter throwing slates, this judge would let the jury hear it...'[1]

David had, in fact, wanted to leave the prison two days earlier but, once he had spent the first night there, he was frightened of reprisals:

> 'One thing I did know was that because I was still there on Monday morning I had a

---

1. 'Strangeways: the truth must be heard'. *Fight Racism! Fight Imperialism!* 115 October/November 1993

problem, because by then the verbal started from the screws and it went around that good kickings were on the menu when you came out. So I didn't. On the Tuesday we got Michael Unger from the *Manchester Evening News* and he came into E wing to assure there would be no reprisals. It was widely reported that a mass eviction was almost on. But it broke down. So by the Wednesday when I felt safe to leave, I left.'

Also to leave the gaol that day were two Category A prisoners, David Judd and Kevin Brown. Both from London and veterans of the prison struggle, they had also spoken with Michael Unger and put the prisoners' demand for no beatings or other reprisals on surrender. It was the last 'mass surrender'; after that only ones, twos and threes would leave. Twenty-six prisoners remained, the so-called 'hard core'.

The Prison Officers' Association announced there were Rule 43 prisoners in North Manchester Hospital suffering from castration wounds. The hospital Public Relations Officer and the consultant-in-charge categorically denied there had been any mutilation of prisoners. This did not stop sections of the press reporting the POA's claim.

Suddenly, having realised far too late that the POA had the media eating out of its hands, the Prison Service began nominating spokesmen and frantically offering interviews. They included a Mr Lockwood, the Governor of Haverigg Prison (itself the scene of large-scale protest in 1988) and a Mr Pilling, then Prison Service Director of Personnel and Finance. Pilling would later replace Chris Train as Director General of the Prison Service, and later still be replaced himself by Derek Lewis, Chairman of satellite TV station, UK Gold.

Thursday 5 April: Woolf Inquiry announced

On the first Thursday of the uprising the Home Office announced the commissioning of the Lord Justice Woolf Inquiry. The Home Secretary told Parliament that all sex-offenders and Category A prisoners were accounted for. And Strangeways prison officer Walter Scott died in Bury General Hospital of a heart attack. He had not been injured in the protest and suffered from a long-standing heart condition.

Tony Bush and John Spencer surrendered; both would later stand trial and be convicted of involvement in the protest. Tony Bush had already attempted to surrender on a previous occasion when he and other prisoners on his behalf pleaded with the authorities to let him leave the roof. Barry Morton describes how the behaviour of the prison officers prevented Tony's surrender:

> 'Tony tried to give himself up but the screws wouldn't let him, saying things like, "I want to see you come out hurt, you bastard" and, "You are one of the many who started this and if you think we're letting you out fit and well, no chance." There's a video which was produced in court taken on day three showing Lord, Spencer, Bush, myself and Azza [Mark Azzopardi] complaining from the roof to the BOV and governors and Bushy and Spencer wanting to surrender and not being allowed to...
>
> 'Finally, Alan got the BOV to get Tony's solicitor to the gaol and to the main barricade and then he and Spencer surrendered into good hands. But it was two days too much; Bushy wanted out the second morning.'

Lowlights of the press coverage of 5 April included *The Sun*'s 'Victims chopped up and dumped in sewers' (citing their source as the police) and *The Independent*'s assurance that against all the odds there were three dead prisoners.

Friday 6 April: 'We fight and stand firm on behalf of humanity'

Paul Taylor attempted to shout out the prisoners' demands but was deliberately drowned out by police sirens. He and others unfurled a new banner which read *We fight and stand firm on behalf of humanity*, along with part of a quotation from Hamlet: 'To thine own self be true, thou cannot be false to any man.' Paul's mother tried to speak to him but was denied access. A report by the Partners of Prisoners Support (POPS) describes the way Lily Taylor was manipulated by both press and police:

Paul Taylor shouting from the roof

'Lillian Taylor agreed to speak to reporters from Sky TV. A series of reports followed showing Mrs Taylor being escorted through police cordons by prison officers so that she could try and persuade her son to give himself up. When the reporters from Sky decided to start reporting from a different angle, Mrs Taylor was quickly dumped by them and was no longer allowed to pass through police cordons to speak to her son. This was a classic case of the press and the authorities deliberately painting a false picture of what was really happening. In reality, family members were being treated in the same manner as other general spectators and were not allowed past police cordons.'

Across the barricades inside the gaol, prisoners negotiated their own surrenders or those of other, younger prisoners. These 'negotiations' were fairly basic. Prisoners who had decided to leave demanded not to be battered when they came out. Other prisoners insisted to the prison officers at ground level that they were not preventing anyone leaving who wanted to, but that they themselves intended to continue the protest. Principal officer Hancox and others replied with comments like, 'You've made your point. Why don't you come out now?' and 'I just don't understand what the protest is about. What are your demands? They've all been met. What more do you want?' Occasionally they tried the 'softly-softly' approach: 'Where are you from, lad? What team do you support?' and when all these overtures met with no movement, resorted to: 'You come out now or you will be brought out eventually, if not by us then by the SAS.'

Andrew Nelson and Mark Petrie surrendered. Andrew would later stand trial twice and, unlike Alan Lord who was convicted on the second occasion, be acquitted both times.

And the band played on...

Overnight on 5 and 6 April, the police outside the gaol began to use loud music to try and force prisoners down. This tactic may have worked in Panama on General Noriega, who loved opera and hated being blasted with Deep Purple, but it didn't work here – despite being treated to Wagner's *Valkyrie* at full blast as well as rock music, a few prisoners danced for the cameras; the rest donned headphones and did their best to ignore it. For two nights the area resembled an outdoor rock festival. *The Observer* of 8 April described how, 'Bright spotlights and strobes are trained on the roof, rock music is intermittently played and a low-flying helicopter buzzes...'

As well as the music, there was the abuse, the war-like hammering on shields, the insults to prisoners and their families, and the ball-bearings catapulted at the roof: all designed to terrify the protesters. Alan Lord says that 'at first the taunts were directed to all but later they began to directly pick inmates to provoke...'

Friday's *Sun* revealed 'Jail Riot Leader is a Rape Monster'. From then on all the tabloids, including the *Manchester Evening News*, referred to Taylor as a rapist. The 'revelation' referred, in fact, to a conviction which was not for perpetrating a rape but for being present in a flat where a rape took place. Prison officers seized on it with glee and began chanting 'rapist' and 'beast' at Paul Taylor in an attempt to turn other protesting prisoners against him. Their behaviour degenerated to a degree where Governor O'Friel was forced to disassociate himself from it, whilst, of course, assuring those prison officers concerned that he sympathised with 'their frustration' at the prolonged siege.

There were many attempts by the media to find dirt about Paul Taylor. Another example was the contention that 'he was on the roof at Risley when the remand centre was ripped apart and later was at the centre of trouble at Durham, where he caused such mayhem that he was sent to Strangeways...' (*Manchester Evening News*). In fact at the time of the 1989 Risley uprising, Paul Taylor was at Strangeways.

David Mellor told TV-am: 'People say the government is on the rack. It should be the prisoners.'

Saturday-Sunday 7-8 April

As gaols around Britain exploded and the Strangeways prisoners listened eagerly to the news on the radio, Governor O'Friel told the press he could not 'rule out bodies' although by that stage he *must* have known that he could. The *Daily Express* quoted a prison officer, who told them that, 'allowing for some margin of error, it now seems almost certain there have been 15 deaths or more'.

8 April was Palm Sunday. Chaplain Noel Proctor pinned a palm cross on the door of the prison, handed others to journalists and conducted a service in the Prison Officers' Mess. In the early evening half a dozen prisoners on the roof of A wing tried their best to shout down to friends, relatives and supporters below, while prison staff activated a siren to drown out their voices. A few hours later a well-aimed slate from the roof of E wing destroyed the camera of a police 'evidence-gatherer'. These detectives were on hand throughout the protest, taking photographs, tape-recording conversations, snooping about preparing the ground for future prosecutions even before it had been determined whether there would be any.

Monday–Tuesday 9–10 April: The day the music died

The loud music carried on until Monday when the Home Office put a stop to it. That morning *The Sun* said 'Jail riot scum must be crushed' and the *Manchester Evening News* 'Riddle of 10 missing prisoners — men could have met gruesome death.' *The Guardian* carried an article by ex-prisoner turned hack-journalist, John McVicar, entitled 'A needless agony of waiting' which advocated in no uncertain terms that the prison should have been retaken by maximum force at the earliest possible opportunity.

On Tuesday 10th four prisoners repulsed a dawn raid via C wing by 50 screws, three of whom were injured — one by a prisoner and two more when one of them fell on top of the other who in turn fell down to the landing below!

Between 8 and 10 April six prisoners surrendered, leaving just 13 men inside the wrecked gaol. Mark Kinsella, one of the two who surrendered on day 10, was quoted by the *Manchester Evening News* as saying that the remaining men had plenty of food left, including rump steak. Other prisoners confirm this:

'When the riot started, inmates who were staying to put forward their say about the system, went round getting plenty of food and stacking it into big carrier-bags and putting them in spare cells or up high on the scaffolding. There was always food. When they stopped the water we had cartons of orange and other drinks. When the meat went off we carried on eating biscuits and chocolate and complan. Even if the protest had gone on even longer than 25 days there wouldn't have been any problem with the food'.

Wednesday 11 April: 'Bazza and Azza' surrender

Three prisoners surrendered on the Wednesday. Two of them, Barry Morton and Mark Azzopardi, were close friends and had been together throughout the protest; the third was a Young Prisoner, Nathan Gaynor. Barry describes what happened:

'We negotiated to have our girlfriends and Nathan's mum and our solicitors, a doctor, BOV and to take photos of our bodies, just in case we got a beating once they left. We made sure our solicitors got a photo as it was a Polaroid and the photo comes out there and then . . .

'We came down the bottom of E wing gates where there were about 30 to 35 riot screws behind a gate with the PO Parry and the SO [Senior Officer] Duncan who we'd asked for, and Gareth Hughes who was my brief and Azza's. When we got there we felt safe . . . They took Azza first, then me, then Gaynor. We saw the doctor, then the police took our clothes and took the photos and put us into strip-cells where our girlfriends came to see us. All this happened while our solicitor was present; then we stayed for about an hour and a half, maybe two hours, until the police escort took Gaynor while Azza and I stayed for about another half an hour. Then they came for me and to my surprise Gaynor was still in the van. They cuffed me to him and went to get Azza.

'While I was waiting I saw about five screws giving Azza sly digs with their legs at the back of his feet. I started kicking the door but got dragged down and I saw Azza being dragged back into the hospital. He was complaining about the cuffs being too tight. They got an escort and took Gaynor and me out of the gaol and dropped Gaynor at Collyhurst and then took me to Stretford police station and put me on my own, Cat A'd up. They didn't beat me while I was there but when I got interviewed I put in a complaint about Azza getting battered after we got promised that nothing would happen . . .

'When they first took Gaynor and put him in the van, our brief went, thinking we were all going, but we stayed that extra half an hour and that's when all the games started. The only comment I made in my interview was about Azza.

'Azza went to Longsight police station from Strangeways. I got a visit the same night from my girlfriend and his, telling me that his hands where he was cuffed were like a balloon.'

Thursday 12 April: 'Coming down on Friday'

It was a calm, sunny day and although the *Manchester Evening News* was still finding screws to talk to about possible bodies, nobody really believed it any more.

On the roof of Strangeways the remaining prisoners sunbathed and there was a general feeling that the revolt was nearing its conclusion; a banner on the roof reading *Coming down on Friday* seemed to confirm this impression. Few people suspected that the protest was only half way through.

Chapter Five

And there were no dead

Friday 13 April: evil abounds

Friday 13th was unlucky for some. Mainly for those on the ground waiting for the protest to end. It was Good Friday and another man of God spoke out: the Archbishop of York this time, saying it was time to end 'this farce' by force. Governor O'Friel claimed that 13 men were still inside the prison. A bad omen and no doubt proof to O'Friel that evil was definitely at work, but in fact only ten prisoners remained. Even at this stage the idea that three were 'unaccounted for' was enough to revive the lust for bodies and blood in some quarters. The prisoners on the roof held up a chalked placard which read *Who's coming to commit murder? Ask the Home Office*.

The prison roof was repeatedly sprayed with water. Following an earlier public insistence by the Fire Chief that 'We are pretty neutral', two 'Green Goddesses' had been provided by the Ministry of Defence. Prison officers were then trained in their use. The Woolf Inquiry heard that the Prison Service Regional Director, Alistair Papps, 'authorised the use of water. . . to create a barrier to stop prisoners entering an area where they might cause injury to staff or further damage to the prison . . . it did not matter if prisoners were to become wet in the process, as long as water was not being used on them directly in a position where they could slip and fall.'

When hosing proved as ineffective a deterrent as the loud music, the prison officers laying siege to the gaol initiated a new tactic. Women officers crept through the prison at night and seductively called out the names of the protesters . . . According to the *Daily Mirror* Paul Taylor had two such 'brave young women' all to himself, one imitating a 'devoted girlfriend, softly moaning his name in the night', the other his mother, urging him to surrender. Ingenious – certainly; disturbing – undoubtedly; effective – apparently not.

Sunday 15 April: prayers and sirens

It was Easter Sunday and publicity-hungry Chaplain Noel Proctor duly prayed for an end to the siege. His prayers were not answered. Instead the central rotunda blazed. The Right Reverend Stanley Booth-Clibborn, Bishop of Manchester, also prayed and suggested force be used to bring about the end.

Wary of the sirens of the previous Sunday, Alan Lord spent the afternoon writing messages on a blackboard and holding it up to those assembled below. Among the spectators was 'John John' Murray's mother, who came every day from Liverpool to see and shout to her son. She was constantly harassed by the police who tried to move her on and prevent her from talking to John. They also followed her around, taking photographs of her for 'identification purposes'.

Monday 16 April: the last seven

On Easter Monday three prisoners became ill with food poisoning, forcing them to surrender. Earl Fahey went to the barricade on F wing to request a stretcher. He and Iain McKinlay then carried Kevin Gee back to the barricade and out of the gaol on it. There were now just seven men holding out: Paul Taylor, Alan Lord, Glyn Williams, Mark Williams, Martin Brian, Darren Jones and John Murray.

Kevin Gee being carried from the prison by Iain McKinlay and Earl Fahey

That afternoon a mini-battle took place between prison officers with fire hoses and two prisoners with slates. Following many dousings, the prisoners attempted to take preventive action by disabling the hose-pipes on the ground. Unfortunately prison officers realised what was afoot and turned the hoses on. A description of events given by a police evidence-gatherer directly contradicts the official statements on how and where such hoses were to be used and confirms that they were directly aimed at the prisoners.

Tuesday 17 April: negotiations

The seven remaining prisoners opened serious negotiations with the authorities to bring the siege to an end. Pressure was growing on the Prison Service from all sides.

To make matters worse, local Manchester businesses had begun to complain loudly about the devastating effect the episode was having on their trade, due to the closure of access routes and the noise and disruption caused by helicopters, sirens, music and water. A leather jacket business 400 yards from Strangeways claimed it had lost £20,000 worth of revenue.

Wednesday 18 April: a good breakfast

Fire-hoses were still spraying enormous quantities of water onto the roof. In a display of defiance the seven remaining prisoners ate a hearty breakfast on the roof and showered in the water spray. Martin Brian, who had already made a roof-top appearance dressed as Worzel Gummidge, treated the onlookers below to an exercise routine including multiple sit-ups and press-ups.

Thursday 19 April: definitely no dead

Governor Brendan O'Friel finally admitted that there were 'no dead'. But Greater Manchester police issued its own 'explosion of evil' statement, saying the riot was the 'most savage incident of its kind ever experienced within the British prison service' and asking for £2 million for policing costs.

Friday 20 April: 'not in my prison yard'

The POA announced that its members could have retaken the gaol on day two if O'Friel had not been prevented from giving the go-ahead by a phonecall from Brian Emes, Deputy Director General of the Prison Service. This row about 'how it was managed' would run and run, often entirely obscuring the real issues which caused the protest.

Prison officers at Walton gaol in Liverpool began refusing to accept prisoners from the Manchester area because of a perceived threat to the safety of staff. Walton was already over its capacity of 930 prisoners, so there was some sense in not taking in any more, but the geographical specification was clearly a case of 'not in my backyard', particularly given that a sizable number of the prisoners housed in Strangeways (including Paul Taylor, Mark Williams, John Murray and Tony Bush) were from Liverpool.

Saturday 21 April: on prescription

It was a warm day; the seven remaining prisoners sunbathed on the roof. Supporters of the Prisoners' League Association and the Revolutionary Communist Group assembled outside the gaol, displaying placards with slogans such as *No reprisals* and *We support the seven!* Relatives of prisoners who had surrendered told the press that the men had been given largactyl in police stations. The police denied giving 'medicine without prescription'.

Sunday 22 April: Waddington visits

The Home Secretary David Waddington did not visit the prison in person until three weeks after the protest began. Perhaps because central Manchester held bad memories for him. Waddington had been Home Office Minister for Immigration while Douglas Hurd was Home Secretary and a major thorn in his side during that period had been the Manchester-based Viraj Mendis Defence Campaign[1] whose members hounded

1. Viraj Mendis was a member of Manchester Revolutionary Communist Group and his Defence Campaign was the highest profile campaign of a large number of Manchester-based anti-deportation campaigns in the mid-1980s. Viraj spent three years living in sanctuary in the Church of the Ascension in Hulme, Manchester, before being deported by force to Sri Lanka in January 1989.

him throughout the election campaign of 1987, disrupting every meeting he spoke at and, at one point, occupying his constituency office at Ribble.

David Waddington did not last very long at the Home Office after Strangeways. He was reshuffled in favour of Kenneth Baker in November 1990 after 13 months in office. He was the first Home Secretary for 20 years to openly declare his support for capital punishment; on retiring from the House of Commons in 1992 he became Lord Waddington and is now Governor and Commander-in-Chief of Bermuda, a British 'dependency' which still has the death sentence.

Booby traps and fires

Throughout the siege POA representatives maintained that the prisoners inside had laid a range of lethal traps to maim or kill any prison officer who came across them while reclaiming the gaol.

Those involved in holding the prison insist that there never were any booby traps. Paul Taylor explains:

'I would like to impress that at no time whatsoever were booby traps laid within the prison; however, we were using our very own psychological warfare in that we convinced the authority of the prison service that we had in fact laid many booby traps on the landings. I touched upon that fact in negotiation by inviting prison officers to come into the prison, to storm the prison at any time they cared to, with of course the awareness of the precarious problems they would have in coming along landings, where I would not explain what traps had been laid. They would then realise that I had not explained what kind or types of booby traps had been made, so they would have to question prisoners coming out.

'We asked prisoners leaving to appear reluctant at first to speak about booby traps, then to tell the Prison Service chiefs that sections of the landings had been taken out on each landing with lino covering the several foot gap, making effectively a lion-trap. Also that there were weights on the underside of landings attached to string-rope on the upper levels to bring them crashing down on the riot squad. None of these things were actually implemented; however, to give foundation further to our claims, we put chairs and tables up against the 'ones' landing doors which prison officers had access to at all times, with eating trays on top so that whenever a sneak-squad came along and through, having opened the door by pulling them, the trays would clatter to the ground and alert those of us remaining to be cautious and pose a threat where they would simply back off in retreat again.'

Alan Lord believes, as do others who were there, that the majority of fires in the gaol were started by prison officers, not prisoners:

'During the first day, numerous fires were set alight, obviously a few by inmates, but speculation has it that prison warders were responsible for some of these and certainly during the days that followed too. I recall one late evening on B wing I'd been on the roof conversing with my relatives and on descending I happened to look through the wire mesh above the "fours" landing and noticed some movement on the right hand side of the landing near the recess and I quickly dropped through the hole in the wire and called: "What the fuck are you doing?" But this figure remained quiet and oblivious to my call and carried on lighting a fire in the middle of the landing. This figure was dressed in black with even the head covered. I knew it was an impostor. There were only seven of us remaining in the siege so I knew it was someone else.'

Chapter Six

End of the siege

Monday 23 April: Alan Lord snatched

Alan Lord was snatched by warders on his way to conduct negotiations. He had been down to negotiate with them many times before and each time been given safe conduct back. This time was different.

Unlike the vast majority of prisoners at Strangeways, Alan Lord was serving a life sentence. He was convicted of murder in 1981 and had spent most of his sentence at England's most northerly dispersal prison, Frankland in Durham, when in October 1989 he was unexpectedly moved away from the 'lifers' programme' there to Garth 'training' prison in Leyland, Lancashire. Alan is certain that this move was a political one and part of a strategy whereby a few long-term prisoners are put into establishments where the atmosphere is volatile to calm it down, essentially by bullying the more angry young prisoners into conforming. He argued unsuccessfully against being moved to Garth and being used in this way.

Alan also wanted to remain in the north east, although his family are from Manchester, because at that time he was planning to marry a woman from Newcastle. Furthermore, he argued that if he had to be taken out of the dispersal system, he should also be decategorised from Category B to C, something the Prison Department said was only possible if he 'behaved' for up to two years at Garth. He was eventually moved from Garth, not back to Frankland, but to Strangeways. As well as the general grievances of the prisoners at Strangeways, Alan had been discussing his personal situation and treatment with the negotiators, Mr Tait and Miss Jones.

On 23 April Alan had arranged to meet Tait and Jones at 3pm in the usual 'no-man's land' area in E wing. They had already met the same morning in the same location and 'negotiations were proceeding on a pendulum but they were negotiating. Not all of their terms were acceptable. Neither were ours.'

Tait and Jones appeared to behave normally, calling up to Alan as he came down to be careful of the rubble, exchanging greetings and beginning to resume the dialogue. Something distracted Alan to his left and he realised he was trapped. During the few seconds it took for the C&R squad to move into E1, he 'gazed through the gate and saw my peaceful negotiators retreating from view.'

Capture by masked aliens

Alan describes his capture:

'I clearly saw two large, full-length protective shields being propelled forward by a large amount of bodies, my estimate would be between 10 and 15. No warning was given or the chance for me to surrender peacefully, considering the odds against me. If vengeance is the right expression, then certainly their conduct warrants that title.

'Once I had been forcibly knocked to the ground by the shields, those behind quite viciously proceeded to punch and kick my chest and back, one or two extending blows to the right side of my face and someone callously decided to compress his boot on my neck, therefore preventing me from inhaling... Once this had proceeded for a few minutes I was forcibly lifted with arms painfully locked out behind my back in a manner I can only describe as a crucifixion and to further the excruciating pain, my wrists were being turned to a near 90 degree angle.

'During this I managed to say: "I want to see Mr Tait". A masked alien replied: "We're in charge now, not Mr Tait" in a threatening manner.

'Again I was quite viciously restrained to the ground (face-down) and sadistically had my clothing ripped from my body. One masked alien took his masochistic imagination further by straddling my left arm and proceeding to press all his body-weight on it... Laughing and taunts were issued back and forth.'

'Trussed up like a chicken'

Alan was carried or dragged to a cell where:

'After initially removing my attire, they tactfully trussed me up like a chicken, legs bent at knees, crossed and forced back towards my head with arms crossed behind my back. Once I was rendered immobile, one masked alien placed his whole body-weight on my appendages. The rest of the official mobsters departed to just beyond the threshold. Then the unknown alien quickly jack-knifed back to the door which was conveniently situated behind me, three to four feet away.

'When the party had gone, I got to my feet. The cell was a strip cell and its interior being concrete from floor to ceiling, the temperature was below 60°F which was a breach of health regulations, not forgetting the fact that I was naked.

'I estimate confinement in this condition at somewhere between 20 and 30 minutes. During that time, many people decided to amuse themselves at the spy-hole with cynical, not to say challenging and derogatory comments but such amusement I chose to ignore...

'The door suddenly opened with force and at that exact moment again a large number of bodies (MUFTI) descended on me with agility, no warning, no instructions given, just a silent onslaught...I would not belittle my dignity by cringeing with fright in the face of such people after experiencing the same vicious treatment in the past...Again I was man-handled into the same position with excruciating force. This time there was a voice: "Lord, listen carefully. We are going to put a white suit on you. Then you are going to have your photograph taken. Is that understood? If you speak or say a word the pain will be worse." This was ironic considering the circumstances didn't permit me to feel anything but pain.

'Once the attire was on, the same procedure got me to my feet and turned me towards the door through which two plain clothes people entered, one sporting a Polaroid camera. Approximately three pictures were taken at various distances ...Having conducted their assignment I was being manipulated to the back wall when someone exclaimed, "The doctor's here."

'Appearing at the door, hands buried in his pockets, the doctor stared and said, "He looks all right to me", then callously walked away! No medical examination was conducted, regardless of my appearance.'

'The bimbos'

'The drama appeared to be finished, or so it seemed, because they were just in their favourite routine of again about-turning me...when it was announced, "The Board of Visitors are here".

'The BOV is an independent body of civilians, employed or deputed by the Home Office to tackle complaints and investigate them. These people I can best describe as "bimbos". In some cases they do make a noble stab at the system but it is obvious this governing group is in collaboration with the walls of shame. Therefore it was not the ultimate shock to see the personal appearance of a male approach me and squat to eye-level and say, "Everything all right?" I refrained from answering. . .

'No sooner had this creature departed than I was forcibly manhandled to the floor. . .

'During my wait for whatever encounter next, I did not brood upon the mistreatment or pain to certain areas of my body. On the con-trary, I calmly dozed off in a standing position

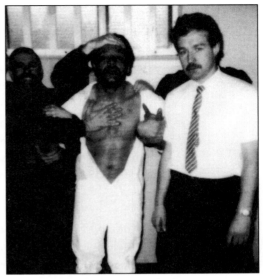

Alan Lord photographed after capture

against the wall. However, again sleep proved difficult, due to characters amusing themselves at the observation hole . . . The person I deem responsible for my abduction had the audacity to appear at the spy-hole and summon the courage to say, "Are you all right? I had no idea that was going to happen. Is there anything I can do, like contact your sister?" . . .

'No apparatus for sitting or laying was in the cell; nor was I given access to the toilet or able to quench my thirst . . .'

Alan estimates that this whole process took between two and three hours, from the point he was captured to his removal from the strip cell and transportation to Astley Bridge Police Station. To get to the vehicle which transferred him, he had to walk a route lined with riot-clad prison officers. On arrival at the police station, Alan went on hunger strike in solidarity with the men still on the roof and maintained this until they came down two days later.

Who do you believe?

The day after Alan's capture the POA and others began to spread conflicting accounts.

Some said the snatch was a complete fluke and he just 'happened to walk right into the middle of our squad, who were carrying out exercises, when he was on the way to speak to negotiators. It was not a trap laid for him.' (Ivor Serle, Strangeways POA Branch Chair.) Others that it was a carefully planned operation, a version of events which eventually became the predominant line and was repeated to the POA conference in May by Peter Hancox who said: 'A decision was taken to recapture Lord. He was recaptured using techniques that had been used earlier by negotiators.' The reason for this fudging was presumably that by this stage the Home Office was desperate to end the protest and stamp on any others which flared up but did not want to appear desperate or seem to have changed tactics from the so-called 'softly-softly' approach.

> '...the Home Office denied that events at Strangeways or Bristol [Pucklechurch] indicated a change in the policy of trying to regain control of the Manchester prison without a dangerous frontal assault.' *The Guardian 24 April 1990*

Lily Taylor arrested

That evening, Lily Taylor was arrested as she said good night to Paul: 'This officer pulled me like a dog, ripped my coat and threw me in the van...He said "You're like your bloody son". At the station I got a pain in my chest and thought I was going to faint...I was pushed in a cell. Oh God, I thought, I won't last the night...The toilet was full and it stank...It was revolting and I felt sick.' She was released after three hours, without charge and told 'there'd been a mistake'.[1]

Tuesday 24 April: And then there were six

According to Alan's sister Eunice Lord, the remaining six prisoners were 'very angry' at the way in which Alan was snatched and 'stayed up another 24 hours in protest'. Mark Williams gives this account of the mood after Alan had gone:

> 'David Bell, the Home Office negotiator, kept contradicting himself, as if in a bid to prolong the negotiations. He would agree to our terms, then he would try and tell

---

1. *Fight Racism! Fight Imperialism!* 95 June/July 1990.

us it was out of his hands, and go back on his word. If it was out of the Home Office's hands – then whose hands was it in?

'I think the final stages were messed around by the Home Office so that our protest could help to divert the public's attention from the Poll Tax revolt that was going on throughout the country. As Alan Lord was snatched after being asked to negotiate on behalf of us all, this made us all more defiant about ending the protest.'[2]

The six agreed, it seems, to come down on Wednesday 25th. Paul Taylor says: 'I never gave my word to come down except on Monday 23 April when I agreed to come down with those remaining at 10am on Wednesday 25 April...at 7.55pm we were given an ultimatum to make a decision by 8.15pm to come down or it would be taken out of the hands of David Bell.'

It was obvious the siege was drawing to a close. Quite how it would end was not yet clear. On the night of 24 April A and D wings blazed in the biggest fires since the protest began. Who started the fires has never been determined; the prisoners are adamant it was not them.

Wednesday 25 April: The last day

Darren Jones was snatched at 10.20am. Aged 17, he had been remanded in custody for joy-riding. On 4 May he appeared at Manchester Crown Court, pleaded guilty and was sentenced to eight months imprisonment; offset against the time he had spent on remand, he was released immediately. Interviewed by *Fight Racism! Fight Imperialism!* two weeks later, Darren said that the prisoners 'wanted it to be a peaceful protest but the prison authority didn't want that...they wanted to use violence...one lad had a snooker ball thrown at him when he was negotiating...He was cut above the eye...People were scared to come down.'

Darren Jones photographed after capture – 'blood all over his face'

2. *Fight Racism! Fight Imperialism!* 96 August/September 1990.

The picture taken of Darren after his capture illustrates his point all too graphically. Three riot-clad prison officers hold this young boy who has blood all over his face. A plain clothes policeman stands at the front, to one side; he is at least six inches taller than Darren. In the files prepared for the courts, this photo is marked 'Surrender of Darren Philip Jones'.

It seems that 25 April was everyone's deadline. Prison officers entered the gaol early in the morning and gradually occupied all the top floor of the prison, leaving the remaining five prisoners on the roof and rotunda. Nevertheless, it took them the whole day to create a situation where the last five had little option but to surrender and even then the prisoners still had the upper hand to an extent and were able to dictate the terms of their exit from the prison.

Paul Taylor sums up the defiance of the protest: 'We did not surrender! We simply made a decision collectively... There were never any leaders. We all simply worked together in preventing for as long as possible the prison being taken back into the control of the prison authority... On the last day we were taking a table-tennis table with table-tennis bats and ping-pong balls on to the roof to put the icing on the cake, so to speak! Wouldn't that have been fun!'[3]

For most of the day enormous quantities of water were sprayed onto the roof. The prisoners remained defiant but were soaked time and again. Preparations were made to spray the roof with detergent so that all but a tiny area would be too slippery to walk on. Screws who reached the roof mocked the banners the prisoners had used to communicate with the public and media throughout the 25 days by putting up their own sign: *HMP in charge – no visits*.

At 6.20pm the final five prisoners – Paul Taylor, Mark Williams, Glyn Williams, Martin Brian and John Murray – made a spectacular departure from the prison in the bucket of a 'cherry picker' hydraulic platform, fists clenched, acknowledging the press and public as they went. It was like a curtain call at the end of a magnificent piece of theatre. And down below hundreds and hundreds of people watched and clapped and cheered and cried. Darren Jones' mother, Shireen, remembers how 'All the prison officers were on the roof and I saw the looks on people's faces... I saw people crying in that crowd...'

3. *Fight Racism! Fight Imperialism!* 96 August/September 1990.

The end of the protest: left to right – Mark Williams, John Murray, Paul Taylor, Martin Brian, Glyn Williams

Prison officers in riot gear reached the roof on the final day of the protest, 25 April 1990

Part Two

Strangeways prison

Chapter Seven

'A sea of abuses'

Strangeways Prison was opened in June 1868 as the county gaol for the Salford Hundreds. It was designed by Alfred Waterhouse, the architect of the Natural History Museum, and built to house 744 male and 315 female prisoners, one to a cell; solitary confinement being the order of the day. In 1963 the women prisoners were transferred to Styal Prison in Cheshire and what had been the women's prison became a Borstal Allocation Centre. In 1965 remand and trial prisoners were moved to Risley Remand Centre but in 1980 overcrowding at Risley led to Strangeways taking remand prisoners once again.

When the alarm went off on 1 April 1990 the prison contained 1,647 men, approximately 925 of whom were convicted adult prisoners, 210 were convicted young offenders and 500 were on remand. The Certified Normal Accommodation figure, ie the number the prison is deemed to be able to contain, was 970. During the 1980s the population regularly reached 1,750, making it the eighth most overcrowded prison in England and Wales. The top figure recorded (in March 1988) was 1,803.

Cords of love...

In 1792 John Brewster wrote in a pamphlet entitled *On the Prevention of Crimes*: 'There are cords of love as well as fetters of iron.' All the reformers of the day were searching for ways to inflict pain and punishment on offenders whilst persuading their victims they were acting justly.[1] Instrumental to the binding of the 'cords of love' was the prison chaplain:

---

1. See Appendix 2 for history of the formation of the modern prison system.

'He would persuade offenders to accept their sufferings as an impartial and benevolent condemnation. He would force them to accept their own guilt. It was he who would enclose them in the ideological prison.' *Michael Ignatieff – A just measure of pain*

Two hundred years later, the role played at Strangeways by the Church of England Chaplain Noel Proctor graphically illustrates both this and the collusion of all who worked in the prison in the brutal treatment of prisoners. Proctor had been at Strangeways for 11 years. Following the events in the chapel he was lauded in the press as a 'brave man' and a 'friend to all'.

In 1979, the first year of Proctor's ministry at Strangeways, a prisoner named George Wilkinson arrived from Durham prison. George had been completely brutalised by his treatment in gaol: by constant moves from prison to prison, breaking his contact with his family and fiancée, whom he was refused permission to marry; by incarceration in specially constructed caged cells at Wakefield and Brixton, and, most of all, by the administration of enormous quantities of drugs (largactyl, librium, valium, sodium amytal, sparine, neulactyl, among others): not to mention the electro-convulsive treatment he was twice given to 'calm him down'.

In Strangeways George 'withdrew' completely; he stopped eating or drinking. After 16 days he was transferred to Walton prison in Liverpool where he began to take fluids again. The damage done to his kidneys was too great, however, and he died the following day.

On the day of George's death a probation officer called at his family's house to tell them that George was critically ill. His brother Louis replied, astonished: 'How can he be critically ill? There's nothing wrong with him.' *Frightened for my life* by Geoff Coggan and Martin Walker contains the following account of Noel Proctor's role in convincing George Wilkinson's family that nothing was amiss while their son and brother was clearly dying:

'Wilkinson's mother, if she hadn't received any letters from him personally between the time of the last visit and his death, had received two letters from the prison establishment. The letters were sent by the prison chaplain in Strangeways, Noel Proctor. The first was sent on 22 November, when Wilkinson had had no food or water for four days. The second was sent on 29 November, when Wilkinson had had no food or water for eleven days and when, if he had been of normal build, he probably would have been dead.'

The second letter reads:

> 'Thank you for your letter which I took down to George and told him of your concern, but he still refused to write to you. So I am writing to let you know that he is all right.
>
> 'However at the moment he will not get out of bed, and he is not talking to anyone. But I am hoping that he will soon come out of this attitude and begin to get on with his sentence. I told him that I would be writing to you and that you sent him your love.'

Fifteen years later Barry Morton was not surprised to hear the story of Proctor's role in the death of George Wilkinson. It was one of the standing sick jokes in Strangeways that when prisoners were assaulted by screws, Noel Proctor would come to their cells afterwards and tell them to cheer up and give them an extra-strong mint.

In his written evidence to the Woolf Inquiry, Proctor said: 'The staff at Manchester prison showed professionalism of a very high quality and I have nothing but admiration for what they came through physically and emotionally during this incident...My opinion regarding the hard-core of prisoners is they consisted of prisoners named Taylor, Lord, Spencer, Bush and Mark Williams. All of these men, I would say, have got mental problems.'

...and fetters of iron

John Bowden, who spent 12 years in long-term prisons in England with many transfers to local prisons on 'lay-downs', has this to say about Strangeways:

> 'Strangeways had long been a prison with a bad reputation in the same category as Wandsworth, Leeds and Winson Green. These were establishments which, apart from their gross overcrowding, poor conditions and "strict" regimes, were felt by prisoners to be the "hard option" or big stick in the hands of the system.
>
> 'While regimes at other prisons were more or less tolerable and some comparatively liberal or relaxed, the regime operating at Strangeways was inflexibly harsh. What particularly distinguished it was its total non-recognition of prisoners' statutory rights and a sea of abuses that flowed from that. Not only were the screws heavy-handed in their treatment of prisoners, but the senior administration of the

gaol, Board of Visitors (BOV), probation officers, governors, doctors and chaplains all colluded and participated in the overall abuse, if not all explicitly, then definitely implicitly by their refusal to ask questions or in any way rock the boat. Strangeways was a place where the rule of law stopped dead at the prison gate and all grades and categories of staff had become tainted by that. As a consequence the atmosphere was one of congealed fear and sometimes terror. Prisoners were controlled by the threat of violence and constantly intimidated into mute conformity. To complain or protest was to invite immediate and awful retribution.

'Strangeways was a place where prisoners were regularly beaten in the segregation unit, where governors and doctors turned a blind eye or actually co-operated with the brutality, where the BOV always provided a cover for the violence and worked hand-in-glove with the screws. Strangeways was what prisoners term "a screws' nick" – a gaol where all power and authority rested with aggressive and bullying screws. To enter Strangeways as a prisoner was to experience almost total dehumanisation and depersonalisation and a constant 24-hour sensation of fear and total vulnerability; you were at the mercy of obvious sadists with the power to do exactly as they pleased with you. The regime at Strangeways had not developed just as a result of tradition and bad staff habits; it had been consciously and deliberately fashioned by senior administrators at the gaol and a conspiracy of silence by people like the BOV, doctors and chaplains protected and defended that state of affairs.

'I arrived at Strangeways in December 1984 on a 10/74 "lay-down". I had already spent over a year on the "ghost-train" alternating between various regimes, some better, some worse, at various gaols. Each regime was designed to test both my level of tolerance to prison discipline and authority and my ability and willingness to protest under certain conditions and restraints. In a "good" segregation unit my co-operation was sought through apparent staff reasonableness and the offer of fair play; in a "bad" unit attempts were made to bully and coerce me. My response to each type of treatment was obviously assessed and analysed and I was, in effect, being subjected to behaviour modification techniques.

'As a consequence of protesting with other prisoners in the notorious Wakefield Control Unit (now F wing) I was moved to Strangeways, I suppose because some aversion therapy was considered appropriate. I spent six weeks in the punishment block at Strangeways and it was probably the worst six weeks of my imprisonment so far – a time of total and complete powerlessness and a reaching of my psychological and physical limits. Struggling to find the will and courage to even complain under a regime of unremitting and constant intimidation is an horrendous experience and I emerged from Strangeways considerably more brutalised and, to a degree, traumatised.'

The prisoners who were in Strangeways in 1990 can confirm that little had changed in the punishment block in the six years since John Bowden's time there. What is more, apart from the outlawing of a few practices such as bread and water diets and flogging, not very much had changed in the worst corners of the prison since the 1960s when Eric Allison first had the misfortune to spend time there. The next chapter is an account of his experiences.

Chapter Eight

Strangeways in the 1960s

by Eric Allison

I was 23 when I first went into Strangeways. I'd got four months for nicking a tray of rings from a jeweller's in Salford. Prior to that my last experience in custody had been three months in a Detention Centre (DC) in 1958. A short sharp shock. When I got to Strangeways in 1965 virtually the only people I knew in there – and there were more than a few of them – were lads from the class of '58. So much for the success of the shock strategy!

Strangeways was a grim place, run mainly by ex-military types. There was plenty of 'fasten that button' and 'tie your tie up properly' stuff.

I vividly recall a scuffle on the exercise yard between two cons. It was only a bit of pushing and shoving, but the screw in charge must have rung a 'one bell' (alarm bell) because a couple of dozen of the 'heavy mob' came rushing out on to the yard. The 'fight' had stopped by then and the two lads were simply mouthing off at one another. The heavies rushed at them, knocked them to the ground, picked them up – one screw to each leg and one for the head – and carried them off the yard, with the ones who hadn't a limb to grab, walking alongside, punching these kids in the back and shouting at them, 'You want a fight, do you, you bastards? We'll give you a fucking fight.' Some fight. Some bastards. This happened in our full view; what would happen when they got to D1, 'the block'?

My 'serious relationship' with Strangeways began in 1968. At Manchester Crown Court Judge Steel gave me four and a half years: three for 'house-breaking' and 18 months for 'the possession of house-breaking implements by night'. Since my previous brief encounter with Strangeways I'd done a 12 month sentence which began at Armley in Leeds. Armley was pretty grim and very dirty and, although in general I remember the atmosphere being marginally lighter than Manchester, I had my first experience of violence from screws since DC days – a knee in the balls for politely objecting to them interfering with my photos during a cell search.

What astonishes me now is that it never entered my head to complain, any more than those of us who witnessed the assault on those two lads in Strangeways – or indeed the victims themselves – thought to complain. There was no point: firstly we would not have been listened to and secondly, once the complaint had been dismissed, the complainant would, invariably, be charged with making a 'false and malicious complaint' against a member of staff: an offence which usually led to a serious loss of remission. This went even further in the case of prisoners assaulted by staff where their injuries were clearly visible. *They* would be charged with assault in order that the injuries could be explained away: 'Had to be restrained, Sir.'

In 1968 Strangeways, as a local prison, served mainly as a holding and allocation centre. Training and long-term prisons were established by now but the allocation system was such that up to and including four years sent you to a training prison; five years or over and it was off to a long-term nick. There was nothing for those in between! So the allocation board told me I could expect to spend at least the next two years in Strangeways. In the event I was to spend the best part of four years there.

Because I thought the allocation board's decision was clearly unfair, I decided to try and do something about it and so embarked on what was later to become almost a vocation – making complaints through official channels. Those channels, although clearly marked, were not easy to navigate because the people who drew up the 'charts' didn't want you to get to your destination. The procedure began like this: step one – complain to your landing officer; if he couldn't/wouldn't help, 'put down' (make an application) to see the Principal Officer; when he couldn't/wouldn't help, put down (the next day, through the landing officer) to see the Governor – a big step.

The Governor at the time was a Captain Davies who did not like hearing applications from convicts; he didn't like convicts at all and made his dislike extremely plain.

Strangeways then was a 'working' prison; everybody worked and it was a punishable offence not to. Around mid-day lunch was served from a hot-plate and prisoners took their food back to their cells where they were banged up for an hour and a half's 'lunch-break'. However, if you had put down to see the Governor, you would be escorted to his office at lunchtime where you would wait outside in a queue until the Captain was ready. In theory he started taking applications at mid-day but in practice he seldom heard the first one until after 12.30 and it was usually gone 1pm when he'd finished. Then all the applicants (because the first had to wait until the last had been heard) would be taken to the kitchen where dinner trays, already loaded, would be cooling on a turned-off hotplate. The food was generally lousy when hot and fresh and it did not improve with age and cooling. Then we'd go and stand outside our cells, usually eat dinner with our fingers, while waiting for the 'landing patrol officer' (who seldom patrolled further than his chair) to come and let us back in. After a few minutes lock-up, it was time to be unlocked again for work.

The actual hearing of the application by the governor proceeded as follows:– The door opens, a screw bawls '*Next!*' loud enough to be heard in Piccadilly Gardens, you walk in, the screw bawls, '*Stand on the mat! Give your name and number to the Governor!*' You do so. Davies or Brown (his deputy) gives a short hiss or snarl which may mean 'yes?' Then you make your application, with the mouthy screw standing right next to you and a braided chief officer standing next to God behind his desk. A nice, relaxed sort of atmosphere to voice your worries, fears, hopes in. And there were many times when the applications were to attend funerals or visit dying loved ones in hospital. One man whose father was terminally ill was told, 'You can either go to see him now or go to his funeral; you cannot do both. You don't have to decide now. Tell your landing officer of your decision when he unlocks you after dinner. That's all. Take him out.' He went to his father's funeral.

If the Governor granted your application – and they did grant some, of course – then the voyage through the waters of complaint was over. When, however, you were knocked back, the journey continued. Now you could communicate with visiting magistrates, write to Her Majesty's Secretary of State for Home Affairs and correspond with your MP – in that order.

First the magistrates: their worships tended to have a wander around the nick about once a fortnight. You could approach them with your complaint. A screw always stood at their side when you spoke. The magistrate would take note of what you said and tell you that he or she would come back to you next time they were in the prison; then they'd make certain that they personally didn't return to the area from where you made your complaint until long after you'd forgotten what you'd complained about.

Following an answer from a single magistrate (and as I said, you wouldn't want to hold your breath waiting for one of them) you could put down to see the Full Board of Visitors. They 'sat' once a month in a boardroom around a very big table: about a dozen of them together with the Governor (a 'dog' – no offence to the canine world but it was/is the term used by prisoners), the Chief Officer, the Senior Medical Officer and the Chaplain (all dogs). You would be marched in and sat at the end of the table with a screw on either side and another one or two by the door. Reeks of independence, doesn't it? These people *never* found in your favour: 'Bloggs, we find that we cannot interfere with the Governor's decision in this matter. It is now open to you to petition the Home Secretary. That is all.' As for petitions to the Home Secretary, there was a widely held theory that they never left the prison and were answered by a clerk in the administration office. Some even joked that they were answered by the night-watchman or the convict cleaner on D1 (a post which had to be held by a grass because of the nature of the brutality that went on in the block.) In fact they did leave the prison and returned, on average, three months later, rubber-stamped with replies similar to previous rejections: 'Bloggs, the Secretary of State, having care...' As with the BOV it was almost unheard of for the faceless Home Office official to interfere with a ruling made by the Governor.

After the petition, the final resort was that you could write to your MP. Apart from one or two notable, shining exceptions, the average prisoner might as well have 'saved his breath to cool his porridge'.

None of these channels were private. Every word you spoke or wrote was open to view by the very people you were complaining about.

Conditions, attitudes, atmosphere

In 1968 Strangeways was overcrowded; in a lot of cases men were three to a cell designed in the 19th century as the minimum space that one man could live in. So you have a room 12 feet by 8 feet containing three beds, three tables and chairs, three piss-pots (if you were lucky, or one or two open buckets if not), and, of course, three men. Those three men are probably incompatible – not all 'criminals' are the same. Imagine it is a weekend night, in the summer, around 9pm. The last slop-out would have been around 4.30-5pm and since then the cell door has been opened once and 'supper' handed in, around 6.30pm. It won't be opened again until 7am. When the men in the cell need to piss or shit after the final slop-out, they do so in the open bucket, or, if they have some newspaper, they spread it on the floor, shit in it, wrap it up and throw the parcel out of the window. The following morning the 'shit parcel patrol' retrieves a hundred, maybe two hundred, such parcels.

The picture was the same in every local prison throughout the country. What varied was staff attitude to the process. In those where the attitude was slightly better, you could ring the cell bell up until about 9pm and be allowed out for a crap. In

Strangeways and those like it, the bell would be ignored, and if you rang it repeatedly and kicked the door in frustration you'd be nicked and lose three days' remission. Furthermore, having failed to get to the recess and opted for the 'parcel' routine, if a yard screw saw which window it was thrown from, you'd be nicked again and lose another three days.

And, of course, if at your adjudication, you said, 'Look, sir, what would *you* do if you were forced to choose between shitting in a bucket or throwing it out of the window?' you'd be charged with using rude and insulting language and, at another hearing, lose more remission. And, if finally at one of these tribunals, your frustration and rage and hate boiled over and you made a lunge past the two screws, who had stood in front of your shoulders throughout the proceedings so the Governor could only see your face, towards Captain Davies or Norman Brown, then you wouldn't have to worry about having a shit for a while because a dozen or so screws would drag you down to D1, the block and kick and punch the shit out of you. Then the visiting magistrate would sentence you to six months in the block, including some days on bread and water.

The conditions were bad – the food lousy, as was access to showers or baths (once a week); the place was crawling with cockroaches; communication with the outside severely limited – one free letter per week plus one purchased from the canteen, if you could afford it; a visit once a month. But even though all this served to annoy, inconvenience and humiliate the prisoners, it never engendered the same rage and hate as the brutal, sadistic and savage behaviour of the staff.

In all the time I spent in Strangeways I saw many appalling things happen. The two worst stand out:

John was down the block for punching a screw and had received a good kicking there. Late one night a screw banged on his door and shouted a message to the effect that his brother was dead. The lad was silent and the screw repeated the message, whereupon John ran to his door, shouting 'Which brother?' One screw shouts back, 'Find out in the morning, you cunt!' Can you imagine what he went through that night, wondering which brother it was, hoping it was one or the other and then feeling guilty afterwards? He was a changed man afterwards, became very withdrawn; several years later he committed suicide.

Barney was remanded in custody to Strangeways. His daughter was married to a

Strangeways screw but Barney kept quiet about that for a while. One night Barney blew his top at the incessant bullying one of his two cell-mates continually meted out to the other and demanded to be moved. He was unlocked and escorted to D1, where he spent the night in the 'strong-box'.

The next morning six screws came in and proceeded to beat him black and blue using fists, feet and sticks. During the assault, Barney screamed out that his son-in-law worked there. The beating stopped. The staff withdrew. Barney was moved to hospital where his wounds were tended, and then to Risley Remand Centre. Barney was then 57 years old; he was 5' 2" tall, with a deformed spine and severely asthmatic.

The screws

In the late 1960s and later, I would split the screws at Strangeways into three groups: the first being the insignificant minority who treated prisoners as human beings (looking back I can count three men who belong in this category) and the other two of which were 'dogs': the 'out-and-out dogs' and the 'ordinary dogs'. The former were usually the 'heavy mob', (first on the scene when the alarm bell went); the physical bullies and sadists who actually handed out the beatings and kickings and were not ashamed of it. Like all bullies, they were cowards, and operated at a ratio of several screws to one prisoner. They joined the Prison Service to bully and get away with it. They strutted the landings in big heavy steel-capped boots and slashed the peaks on their caps. Some of them proudly wore National Front insignia on their uniform – in a prison with a large ethnic minority population. The 'out-and-out dogs' were a small group but they terrorised the entire gaol. In my day the 'dog of all dogs' was a man called Kearns, and when he came to the end of his reign, there were plenty of others waiting in the wings, men such as Shires, Baldwin, Brown, Wright, Duffy...

The 'ordinary dogs' were a much larger pack. They seldom abused prisoners physically but they abused them all the same. They were the ones who would tell you to 'fuck off' many times a day and nick you when you told them to do the same; or, worse still, nick you for telling them to fuck off when you hadn't even done so. They would plant 'contraband' in your cell when they searched it, regularly invent 'crimes' they'd witnessed, fit you up for any breaching of the disciplinary rules – and what rules... it was an offence to lend or borrow a newspaper; it was an offence to stand on a chair at your window in your cell and speak to the guy next door or above you; it was an offence just to stand on the chair and look out of the window. While I was in

Strangeways dozens of men lost dozens of days of remission every single week. I lost months of it on that sentence and when I saw the men on the roof on 1 April 1990 I knew *exactly* why they were doing this. Strangeways hadn't altered much since my day.

Chapter Nine

The prison officer's tale

John Sutton was a prison officer at Strangeways between 1975 and 1985, and testified to both the Woolf Inquiry and the trials of Strangeways protesters at Manchester Crown Court. To the court he described how, with only three months training, he became a qualified hospital officer, entitled to inject prisoners with the 'liquid cosh'. A doctor had to authorise the injection but did not have to be present and it was common for the doctor to give his authorisation by telephone and sign the papers the following day. When asked about the quantities of largactyl used, he spoke of 'pints of the stuff in great bottles'.

Sutton wrote an article for *The Guardian*, based on his submission to the Woolf Inquiry. After its publication, the few prison officers he had maintained contact with since leaving employment at Strangeways ceased to speak to him. The article gave a thumbnail sketch of life for a new prisoner entering Strangeways for the first time:

'Locked in a 10 feet by seven feet cell, no toilet, bars and grill at the window, for at least 20 hours each day...Inside the cell are two other people, total strangers...These men may smoke, play loud music on the radio, break wind, urinate, defecate, often into newspapers which they then force out through the bars and grills of the sealed window, masturbate, shout and bang on the doors...These men to you are an unknown quantity; some inmates suffer the indignity of homosexual rape yet dare not complain. Your cell-mates could be seriously psychiatrically disturbed, high on drugs or suffering from alcoholic symptoms, hallucinations, severe withdrawal pains, outbursts of violence. They may be awaiting hospital care and so on. The door shuts and you are in . . .

'Every hour of the day you are being watched. The cell door has a Judas hole, eyes without faces peer in at you . . . Male eyes, female eyes, whilst you try and eat, sleep, read and take care of nature's functions . . .'

Out of the cell there is no more privacy than in it:

'The toilets have open urinals, so all can observe you urinating. The staff, including the newly instituted female officers, watch you, observe you as you empty the stools and stale piss from 24 hours of incarceration behind that door . . .'

In his evidence to the Manchester Crown Court John Sutton told how prison officers would rip up prisoners' out-going mail instead of posting it and destroy incoming letters but cynically give the prisoner the empty envelope. He described the 'food-free diet' which certain officers would implement for a day or two against prisoners whom they disliked. He talked of prisoners deliberately placed in cells with their worst enemies, of food left to go cold or urinated in by the staff before being given to prisoners. And he described the naked violence meted out to prisoners both by staff and by proxy: 'There were a couple of prisoners used for this at Strangeways, who would be allowed to go round the landings. If the staff felt that somebody needed the treatment, they would have a word with this guy and the next thing you'd know, is you'd find a particular inmate in the recess with a few teeth missing or blood pouring from his face.'

He described one incident of staff violence where:

'three inmates barricaded themselves into a prison cell and were intimidating the staff by shouting abuse at them . . . They got what they called the MUFTI squad; they got the staff dressed up in the outfits with all the gear on and began to jack off the cell door with a hydraulic jack. As they were doing this, the inmates could be clearly heard pleading with the staff, "Right, we'll come out; we have had enough of this." But the response . . . from the staff was, "If you were going to come out, you should have done it some time ago. It's too late now you bastards."

'The door was jacked off and the three inmates were dragged down to the block. They had their clothes stripped off them and I intervened, as the hospital officer, as the staff were taking turns, running along and kicking this particular man, whose teeth, at this time, had been broken, and he was covered from head to foot in boot polish and bruises that had bounced off the shoes of the staff.'

During his time at Strangeways, John Sutton attempted to set up an alternative union to the POA. It lasted about nine months. As a dissident voice, threatening the status quo, he was punished unofficially, both by being removed from his normal duties and made to spend three months at a time on gate duty, opening and closing the front gate all day, and more seriously by physical assault from his colleagues. He was violently attacked on several occasions and finally left the prison service on the advice of his doctor. He has written the following account of the breakaway union's rise and fall for this book:

PFF – the breakaway trade union
by John Sutton

The argument was simple: senior prison service officials with managerial responsibility for policy decision making should not be members of the same trade union as the basic 'blue collar' workers. A serious conflict of interest exists between those who actually do and those who actually don't. It is an all too obvious truth that positions of power and authority are, especially within institutions, invested in those most likely to maintain the status quo. The problem within the Prison Service being that this particular status quo involved the systematic abuse of prisoners' and their gaolers' human rights.

During the mid to late 1970s Her Majesty's prison system filled to bursting point with gaols, such as Strangeways, holding inmates in conditions that were a clear affront to human dignity. The officers of such prisons were, at that time, required to work compulsory overtime. This meant that staff could, and often did, work 13 days out of 14. The shift system included a day which began at 7am, terminating at 9pm. During those 14 hours, for which you were only paid for $12^3/_4$, a basic grade discipline prison officer could expect duties involving long periods of patrolling landings, supervising exercise/visits/workshops/bathing/canteen etc. The stress factors linked into those mundane duties did not register on the senior officials whose direct orders included instructions to lock adult members of the human race into cells 12 feet long by 8 feet wide containing no toilet facilities, for periods of ten or more consecutive hours. Often this method of containment, or human warehousing, clearly contributed to the physical and mental decline of those subjected to it. The conditions were deplorable.

As a serving prison officer employed on discipline duties, I had to undertake certain tasks that, had Strangeways been a prisoner of war camp, would have contravened the

Geneva convention. The insanitary conditions, with 200 or more inmates sharing four toilets, bathing once a week or less, three to a cell, locked in for 90 per cent plus of the time, created an intolerable regime of oppression maintained by intimidation and the threat of violence. That system subjugated not only the unfortunate prisoners, but also the staff, who had no choice but to comply. I tried to change all that. I stood up and said that if we treat prisoners like animals then we should expect them to respond as such.

A prisoner may create quite a lot of waves, metaphorically speaking, using the official channels: letters to the Home Secretary/Board of Visitors/solicitors and legal representatives/MPs or whoever you can think of. Not that these waves are likely to wash away the complex system of red-tape procrastination that effectively reduces such complaints to pointless exercises designed to camouflage the blunt truth. An officer, who is ostensibly part of the team, can only seek to redress a wrong through either his trade union or by direct representation to his line manager. In the prison service this amounted to the same thing; the POA was at the time dominated by senior management officials who were working hand-in-glove with the Home Office Prison Department. Junior staff were unrepresented. The system which abused inmates also abused the staff and to challenge it was the equivalent of signing one's own death warrant.

The Prison Force Federation (PFF) was born out of anger at the lack of representation for non-supervisory grade prison officers. To make any form of representation against a real or construed wrong invited retribution. Prisoners will recognise the syndrome as Insult-Action-Reaction-Block. As an officer the same series of interactions conspired and colluded to confuse and control – the ethos of the institution being best expressed by the 'I'm in charge, you will obey or else . . . !' attitude adopted by those selected and promoted by the Home Office to maintain the status quo. This rule by intimidation was supported by the POA whose senior branch officials (chairman and secretary) were Principal Officers with responsibility for allocating duty work schedules and reporting on junior staff. Complain to them about working conditions and matters really started to deteriorate. Omnipotent demi-gods have an instinctive dislike of underlings who dare to question the oracle of oppression. In 1979 I and a considerable number of like-minded officers tried to form a new breakaway trade union to represent the workers in HM Prisons. This is the true story of how we failed.

We placed a small advertisement in a major Sunday paper asking if 'blue collar' prison staff were interested in a new independent trade union. Responses came from all over the country with many gaols asking for immediate action. Clearly we had touched a nerve. I was elected General Secretary by the staff at Strangeways and, with the kind help of two solicitors, drafted the submission to the Certification Officer in London. By February 1980 the PFF was a properly constituted trade union. The media were excited by the prospect of more trouble inside Britain's prisons and the BBC included the inaugural meeting of the PFF in its award-winning documentary *Strangeways*. Local TV and radio interviewed me. The boat began to rock and before I was able to establish a functional local committee the Governor had charged me with a serious breach of Home Office regulations and disciplinary proceedings were instituted against me. I was, as are all serving prison officers, bound by the Official Secrets Act. Those who saw Rex Bloomstein's documentary, will perhaps remember the rather unedifying sight of HMP Manchester's most senior officials sitting in the Governor's office attempting to find a suitable offence to charge me with.

The PFF was invited to speak at a meeting convened for officers of HMP Liverpool; the day I was due to attend the Governor and his Chief Discipline Officer called a full staff parade. All officers were cautioned that to attend the PFF recruitment lecture was, in itself, sufficient to terminate the individual's membership of the POA. John Sutton was said to be really a member of Militant Tendency and an agent of the ultra-left-wing revolutionary movement. Such utter nonsense scared the staff away. It was of course pure propaganda; disinformation techniques haunted our campaign. In Liverpool, Sutton was a raving revolutionary out to destroy the peace of our nation by disrupting the prison service; at Risley, the PFF were a bunch of National Front nutters determined to institute a policy of ethnic extermination. This clap-trap worked wonders; within six months even the founder members, officers who had helped draft the constitution of the PFF, were convinced John Sutton was paid by either Colonel Gaddafi or Colin Jordan. It was impossible to continue. Officers I had known for many years refused to speak to me and the Manchester branch of the POA presented a motion to conference that I be banned. At Strangeways they openly attempted to have me locked out of the gaol. Game, set and match to the terror machine. POA 1 PFF 0.

Trying to intellectualise the underlying reasons for our failure is far easier now than it was then. In retrospect one has the benefit of an enhanced overview, the control system is clarified and it is clear that the odds against overturning a well-established oligarchy using reason and argument were overwhelming. Prison officers are, in the majority of cases, concerned with certain specifics: A) money, B) security of employment, C) pensions. Anything beyond ABC is unlikely to grab the imagination of an average gaoler whose main considerations are maintaining a reasonable standard of living for themselves and their families. Secondary considerations, such as the abuse of prisoners' rights, are never likely to enter the agenda.

If we accept that gaolers are motivated by ABC it becomes increasingly apparent why the breakaway trade union failed. The incentives offered by the PFF were, on reflection, totally insufficient. All we could offer was decent, honest representation in defence of basic human rights for prison officers. The argument that staff were being reduced to the level of mere automatons, required to abuse and defile their fellow human beings, never really stood a chance. In the scheme of life to a gaoler, inmates are simply an essential, even unpleasant, evil. In the world of Strangeways and prisons like it the staff work for wages; if one understands that, then all else falls naturally into place. Those who best comply with the existing plot are promoted and get higher wages. The whole is a self-perpetuating system based on maintaining the method by which the staff are remunerated; anything else is a dream. As the man behind the answer that never was, I can only say that at least I dared to dream . . .

When John Sutton was asked in court during his evidence for the Strangeways protesters how he viewed the Prison Department now, he replied, 'From a distance, thankfully.'

Part Three

A revolting system

Chapter Ten

A system in revolt

The uprising at Strangeways gave courage and strength to prisoners around the country. Between 1 and 25 April 1990 there were protests at over 20 gaols.

1 April: Hull

The news of the Strangeways revolt spread around the country at high speed. By Sunday afternoon prisoners were glued to their radios. The first 'copy-cat riots' or solidarity actions, depending whose version you listen to, began that very day. Dave Noble wrote this account of what happened at Hull that afternoon and how quickly and viciously the participants were dealt with:

'An estimated 100 prisoners sat down on the exercise yard; all were remand prisoners. They stayed in the yard for about 30 minutes and five prisoners got on to a small roof. They came down immediately. Out of this five, three of them were in front of the governor and placed in solitary confinement for three days, lost seven days remission and seven days privilege. The other two were kept in segregation on Good Order And Discipline – one of them was still there 21 days later. The other one was shipped out to HMP Frankland. My two co-accused have been in segregation for 21 days for just being involved in the sit-down.'[1]

1. 'Brutality in Hull prison' – Dave Noble. *Fight Racism! Fight Imperialism!* 95 June/July 1990.

Gartree

Disturbances were also reported at Gartree prison in Leicestershire, Kirkham, an open prison near Blackpool, and Rochester prison in Kent. In fact, the Gartree protest was not a 'copy-cat' action by any stretch of the imagination as it had already been in progress for three days but had not of itself commanded more than scant media attention. Paul Ross, who was at Gartree at the time, describes what took place:

'On 28 March three men staged a roof-top protest to highlight the inhuman/oppressive conditions that all prisoners have to endure throughout their incarceration and while on the roof placards were unfurled declaring: Justice for Alan Byrne, Roy Ivers, Charles Campbell, Gerry (Superglue) Miller, Winston Silcott, John Cominzcy, Bob Maynard, Graham Gillard, The Bridgewater 4 and the Birmingham 6 etc (sorry if I've missed anyone).

'The Home Office/media declared the whole demonstration solely a publicity exercise for the Birmingham 6 and railroaded the primary issues, ie, 1) that all prisoners had been stopped from wearing their own clothes on a visit because someone had escaped from Leicester prison, 2) that Gartree is the only nick in the country which has got six cameras in the visiting room that intimidate people's visitors, 3) publicity for all prisoners' grievances and injustices.

'Three of the Birmingham 6 were at Gartree at the time and realised that the three men on the roof were up there for the aforementioned purpose and as a result of approximately 30 men who had guarded/protected them from the screws and dogs while they scaled the razor wire to reach the roof. The 30 odd men then returned to their wings and demolished them to the best of their ability while simultaneously burning their prison uniforms and throwing them out of the windows. They were subsequently dispersed throughout the system while the ones on the roof stayed up for roughly a fortnight.'[2]

2. Paul Ross was moved from Gartree to Bristol on 30 March; then, when that prison erupted, he was again moved to Lincoln on 10 April and subsequently to Wandsworth on 3 May. This account of events at Gartree is part of a letter Paul wrote to *Fight Racism! Fight Imperialism!* and which was stopped under Prison Standing Order 5B 34 (9)d, which states that a prisoner cannot send out 'Material which is intended for publication or for use by radio or television (or which, if sent, would be likely to be published or broadcast) if it refers to individual inmates or members of staff in such a way that they might be identified.' A second copy was later smuggled out from HMP Frankland.

2 April: Long Lartin

The day after Strangeways exploded there were minor disturbances at Lindholme, Low Newton and Bedford gaols and a major incident at Long Lartin maximum security dispersal prison in Worcestershire. What happened at Long Lartin was not 'copycat' and can't really be described as a 'riot' either. In fact it was an escape attempt which had been planned for months.

All of the men who planned the escape were serving long sentences; several were framed prisoners, one was an Irish Prisoner of War. Waiting for the arranged day to come around, they watched enthusiastically as it 'went off' in Trafalgar Square on 31 March and cheered still more the following day when the Strangeways prisoners raised a *Smash the Poll Tax* banner. And they became aware of the climate in which they were making their bid for freedom: 'If Strangeways was shaking the prison system . . . then this escape would, if it succeeded, make it crumble.'

On Monday morning cells on all the wings at Long Lartin were searched. It was pure persecution as the prisoners were jubilating over Strangeways. Prison officers had not been tipped off about an escape attempt; they were searching for illicit alcohol and were so determined to find it that they never noticed any of the sections of a 24 foot long ladder which were waiting to be assembled!

The escape attempt began, later than planned, at 8.45pm. Andrew Russell and Alec Sears climbed out of a window on C wing and clamped shut the gates which could give staff access to the compound they were entering. The three other C wing prisoners taking part then joined them, the ladder was assembled and the men headed for the perimeter fence. They were then joined by the three participants from B wing. Andy Russell tells the story:

> 'B wing directly looked onto the stretch of the compound where we were to be going from. Because of this we had to have people in the TV rooms in case anyone saw from the windows and attempted to tip off the screws. We didn't have to worry; everyone was 100 per cent!
>
> 'I've since been told that someone shouted out, "Look, the screws are doing a security manoeuvre again." Everyone looked out and soon someone retorted. "That ain't the screws, it's C wing out on manoeuvres!" Everything then went deathly silent as everyone realised what they were witnessing and that B wing were also "on manoeuvres".
>
> 'We started to cut through the fence and it wasn't too long before we could hear

the screws banging the doors in frustration as they couldn't get to us. We had actually locked the gaolers into the gaol!

'Next, four screws appeared from A wing. [The prisoner whose task it had been to clamp the access doors from A wing had forgotten to do so.] As they came across the compound the people viewing the escape from B wing realised the balance was shifting and spontaneously erupted. Windows were kicked out which fell onto the compound, the wing was taken and as much mayhem as possible was caused.

'The four screws approached us, followed by two more with dogs... We had now cut through the fence and I went through and pulled the ladder through. The rest followed while Alec held the cut fence apart to allow the others to get through easily... The screws came up behind and rained truncheon blows down on his head until it split. Alec screamed at everyone to go as he wasn't going to be able to get through. We erected the ladder but as it reached its full height and was just about in position, the wind caught it, the ladder bowed and the wood split and broke at its weakest point...'

It was a tragic ending to a valiant attempt. Those involved had no choice but to surrender. They were all moved to the block and quickly shipped out of Long Lartin on 'laydowns' to various gaols around the country. Some were sent to Bristol prison and were immediately caught up in the riot there. Prisoners on B wing who had shown solidarity were treated in the same way. Enormous quantities of prisoners' clothing were burned and property smashed by prison officers. The prison was later forced by a series of writs in the small claims court to recompense prisoners for this damage.

4 April: Durham, Winchester and Wandsworth

At Durham a prison officer was held hostage for 24 hours. At Winchester 'trouble' was sparked off by the transfer of Strangeways prisoners and again at Wandsworth there was an incident, described in *The Guardian* as 'four Strangeways inmates transferred to Wandsworth try but fail to incite a riot'.

6 April: Glen Parva

A disturbance took place involving 50-60 prisoners in the remand section of Glen Parva Young Offender Institution and Remand Centre in Leicestershire. The prisoners' grievances included bad food, lack of association and long hours locked up in their cells; the Remand Centre was seriously overcrowded with 330 prisoners in accommodation designed for 192.

7-8 April: The weekend of mass protest

The weekend of 7-8 April was the time of militant action on a mass scale. Protests of varying size took place and, unlike those at Gartree (where the three men on the roof were still standing firm) and Long Lartin, which had taken place independently, most were in direct response to Strangeways. Prisoners around the country saw it as a time of common protest against common grievances.

At Armley in Leeds there was a sit-down protest, following the arrival of over 100 men from Strangeways. Armley had for several years been infamous as Britain's most overcrowded gaol and had an appalling record of suicides among young remand prisoners. While the ball of fire that was Strangeways ricocheted around the prison system, four Armley screws appeared in court in Leeds charged with assaulting prisoners and perverting the course of justice. Unlike their victims, they were not remanded in custody but granted unconditional bail.

Dartmoor: 'Strangeways, we are with you!'

At Dartmoor 100-120 prisoners joined a large-scale protest, wrecking the whole of D wing. Twelve of them got on to the roof of C wing. They carried a banner which read *Strangeways, we are with you*.

Dartmoor prison was built by and housed French prisoners of war in the Napoleonic War in 1809. It was first used as a civilian prison in 1851. One hundred and eight years later a government White Paper declared that Dartmoor was nearing the 'end of its serviceable life' and when Albany gaol on the Isle of Wight was first commissioned in 1961 it was intended as a replacement for 'the Moor'. The May Committee in 1979 again recommended closure, describing the isolated, insanitary, cold buildings as 'nowadays simply against nature'.

Following the 1990 uprisings, the Woolf Inquiry Report (published in 1991) held back from recommending closure, but only just. It found that, 'On the assumption that the need for prison accommodation is such that Dartmoor is required to house prisoners, then drastic action is required if Dartmoor is to be retained as a prison establishment...This should be Dartmoor's last chance.' A year later the Home Office published a report by the Chief Inspector of Prisons which it had been sitting on for nine months and which called Dartmoor a 'dustbin' and said once again that the establishment should be given a final chance – to become a 'community prison' for the West Country. 'If such a prison is not wanted then Dartmoor should be closed.' At the time this report was issued Devon and Cornwall police were investigating an alleged racket whereby prisoners desperate to move to any other gaol could pay £250 to prison officers to arrange it.

Following the publication of the Inspectorate report, the Prison Reform Trust spoke out in uncharacteristically strong terms against maintaining Dartmoor prison in any shape or form: 'It is isolated and run down and for 200 years has been dominated by a culture of barbarity and punishment. That culture is all-pervasive and repeated attempts to change it have produced nothing but failure...'

Dartmoor prison is still open.

In 1990 Jimmy Morrison had already served 18 years of a life sentence and was later sentenced to a further two and a half years' imprisonment for his part in the Dartmoor protest. Having completed that term, he is still in gaol, having been told 'unofficially' that the elastic provision of the life sentence is being deliberately stretched to ensure he serves at least six years for being a participant at Dartmoor. He wrote the following account:

'People on the outside don't really understand what it is to be "Nothing". I've been in many prisons myself and I know for a fact that people don't lead lives of luxury behind bars. I can still see in my mind the pain and suffering from the past in Dartmoor. When I first went to Dartmoor I was locked up for weeks...I thought people had rights in prison until I went to Dartmoor. I soon found out that the only rights you had was from someone's fist. I just couldn't believe it at first. In 16 years in prison I'd never seen animals like the ones in this establishment before.

'In Dartmoor the air smelled of sewage all the time. When a lifer is locked up 22 hours a day on the wing, it can get very depressing. The history of this prison is power and brutality and cheap thrills.

'It can be an unnerving experience when you first go down the Seg Unit at Dartmoor, as I found when I came down off the roof. His fist smashed into my back and my head. I was so tired when I came down, so I just ignored him. Looking back on it now, it was a fatal mistake, coming down first. I call what happened to me that day brutality. When I was on the wing, prison officers always seemed to get an incredible kick out of seeing human beings hurt. If you're not a survivor or mentally tough, the only way out of this brutality is suicide. Which happens, believe me.

'The most frightening thing about the brutality in Dartmoor is they get away with it. The governor and doctor put up smokescreens to hide it.'

Bristol

Thirty-two Dartmoor prisoners were moved to Horfield prison in Bristol where, following their arrival, there was another major protest. Three wings were taken over by up to 400 prisoners and held for two days. Although the official explanation is that the protest was begun by the Dartmoor prisoners (and there is probably some truth in it) another factor in sparking revolt was that it was the tenth anniversary of the St Paul's Uprising. St Paul's is a predominantly black area of Bristol and the uprising there in 1980 was the precursor to the 1981 risings in most British inner-cities. Staff might have been unaware of the anniversary; prisoners certainly would not have been. And as Paul Ross, who was moved from Gartree to Bristol on 30 March 1990, explains: 'Bristol prison is notorious for racially motivated assaults on prisoners by the staff'.

Two years later, in the summer of 1992, remand prisoners at Bristol threw rubbish and shouted abuse at Princess Anne when she unveiled a plaque at the re-opening of the riot-damaged A wing.

In April 1993 the Chief Inspector of Prisons published a report on Bristol which concluded:

'In April 1990, the month of the riot, Bristol was an overcrowded local prison with few facilities for inmates. When we inspected, in June 1992, apart from the redevelopment work, little appears to have changed.'

Cardiff, Hull and others

At Cardiff 130 prisoners destroyed cells and surrounding areas for three hours. Again Cardiff was (and still is) a decaying, putrid pre-Victorian dump. Built in 1827, it was infested with cockroaches and rats; it was grossly overcrowded and prisoners had to queue to slop out.

There was a 20-hour rooftop protest at Stoke Heath Young Offenders' Institution.

Brixton, Stafford, Pentonville and Shepton Mallet prisons all had 'incidents' and at Hull 110 prisoners staged a second sit-in in the exercise yard. Dave Noble reports again:

'On 8 April another disturbance took place by the remand prisoners. Again it was blown out of proportion by Mr Wheatley, the Governor, who already had teams of officers marching around the prison dressed in brown boiler suits and full riot gear, helmets, batons and shields. Sixty riot police were placed outside the prison, all roads around the jail were cordoned off by the police and police with binoculars assembled on the docks. One prisoner who I managed to speak to said, "The riot police gave everyone on the yard an order, 'Either you come out now or we'll come in and drag you out'".'

9 April: The Verne, Bristol and Dartmoor

Prisoners smashed the windows at The Verne Category C prison in Dorset; Bristol was recaptured by force by the authorities and, following the surrender of the other prisoners who had gone up with him, one lone man, Joseph Collins, remained on the roof at Dartmoor, demanding a transfer nearer to his home in Liverpool.

10 April: Shotts

At Shotts, Scotland's so-called 'model prison' which has gone up time after time in its short history, 40 prisoners took over B Hall, holding a prison officer hostage for 24 hours. Stephen Windsor, who was in Shotts for most of 1989, thinks that the protest there had more to do with the previous ones at the same establishment than with those in the rest of the country:

'The riot was a continuation of earlier ones and such was the regime that prisoners were simply not going to take any more. It might sound a bit strong to some but the riot was promoted by the staff . . . in order to put a purge on prisoners . . .'

11 April: Dartmoor – 'Stop Brutality!'

Joseph Collins put up a banner which read *Stop Brutality*. Three prisoners from A wing climbed onto the roof in solidarity with those who had surrendered and were now in the punishment block and stayed there for two and a half hours. They agreed to come down after negotiations with a Senior Officer who promised they could return to their wing and would not be sent to the block themselves; a promise which was not kept.

12 April: Swansea

Two teenage remand prisoners barricaded themselves in their cell for 17 hours. The barbaric conditions under which young prisoners at Swansea were kept would be dramatically brought to public attention in July 1990 by the suicide of 15-year old Philip Knight.

14 April: Dartmoor

After eight days on the roof, Joseph Collins finally surrendered.

In the summer of 1991 17 men stood trial at the notoriously right-wing Winchester Crown Court for their part in the Dartmoor protest. David Palmer was acquitted after the prosecution evidence, on grounds of mistaken identity; the others were convicted. Joseph Collins was sentenced to three years' imprisonment, Jimmy Morrison to two and a half years', others to similar sentences.

22 April: Pucklechurch

The last of the so-called 'copy-cat protests' took place at Pucklechurch remand centre near Bristol. Between 80 and 100 remand prisoners, all aged under 21, took to the roof and remained there for 18 hours. These young, unsentenced prisoners were subjected to extreme overcrowding, 19-hours a day lock-up, slopping-out, 15-minute visits, dirty kitchens, infrequent changes of clothing, little opportunity for work or education, bad exercise facilities and no assistance with preparing legal casework. In short, it was very similar to Strangeways.

The Pucklechurch protest was brought to an end by maximum force at 1pm on Monday 23 April. Two squads of prison officers in riot gear stormed the prison. Surrendering prisoners were beaten with truncheons. They were stripped naked and left in bare cells for three days. Their clothing and property were never returned to them but left in plastic bags, drenched from hosing, to moulder in the corner of a workshop.

Prisoners on the roof at Pucklechurch

23 April: Full Sutton

At Full Sutton dispersal prison in York the authorities were absolutely determined to show that they were in charge and here there would be no dissent. 400 prisoners were confined to their cells for the stated purpose of a 'weapons and drugs search'. The lock-down went on for five days and on the first two it was total, 24 hours a day, breaking Prison Rule 27 which provides for 'exercise in the open air for not less than one hour'.

Prisoners fightback

The overwhelming majority of prison protests and revolts which took place in April 1990 were in local prisons, the overcrowded dustbins which had the worst conditions and the most repressive regimes. The Prison Service had never bothered too much about improving these, as the relatively short sentences being served by most local prisoners meant a constantly changing prison population much less likely to protest. All that had changed; potential dissent was everywhere. Unlike long-term prisons which are far from towns or cities, local prisons are in the middle of cities for all to see; they contain the sons, brothers, husbands and friends of people who live nearby. The possible consequences of continued disruption in these gaols and the potential threat of accompanying working class solidarity (the anti-Poll Tax riot of 31 March was also being repeated in smaller form around the country) sent shock waves through Whitehall and Westminster and forced 'reform' to the top of the agenda.

Chapter Eleven

Lies and liars:
the press and the POA

The Prison Officers' Association (POA) is the trade union to which the overwhelming majority of serving prison officers belong. It deservedly has the reputation of being a vicious, racist, anti-working class organisation. At the 1980 TUC Conference the POA put a motion calling for a referendum on the re-introduction of capital punishment; fortunately there was no seconder and the motion fell.

As John Sutton has graphically described in Chapter 9, the POA is an integral part of the prison system. But it has an agenda which is not identical to that of the Prison Service. Its overriding concern in all matters is the welfare of its own membership. Concern for prisoners' welfare is voiced by POA spokesmen in smaller or greater measure purely according to how the welfare of prison officers is affected.

The battle cries of the POA are 'under-staffing' and 'danger to our members'. Under-staffing is a complete myth. Strangeways did not go up because there were too few staff but because the place was a dump and the staff who were there ran it for their own convenience, meting out frequent and extreme brutality to prisoners. While the prisoner population dropped from its all time high in 1987 over the three years which followed, the number of prison officers increased by 20 per cent. It had already increased by 136 per cent in the 20 years 1965-85, in contrast to a 46 per cent rise in the prisoner population over the same period. Yet the regimes they presided over did not improve; in the majority of cases they deteriorated. As the ratio of staff to prisoners increased (1:2.95 in 1965, 1:1.8 in 1985) there was less education, less training, less work and less physical exercise available for prisoners.

Brutality by prison officers against those they guard is common. The few cases which reach the courts or public attention – such as the beatings of prisoners who took part in the Hull protest in 1976, the murder of Barry Prosser in Winson Green in

1980, the violent assault on John Bowden in the same gaol in 1989, the murder of Omasase Lumumba in Pentonville in 1992, the various assaults on prisoners at Armley for which four officers were facing charges even as Strangeways blazed — expose a general attitude of sadism and thuggery. And it is certain that they are only the tip of an iceberg.

The POA is renowned for its racism. In 1988 just 0.6 per cent of prison officers were black. In the 1970s many POA members openly flaunted their membership of the National Front. An inquiry by the anti-fascist magazine *Searchlight* named Strangeways, Wandsworth, Pentonville and Dartmoor as the gaols where the evidence of organised fascism was incontrovertible. At Strangeways 40 per cent of the staff were estimated to be active in the National Front. Irish Prisoner of War, Raymond McLaughlin, described a 'cooler' ('lay-down') in Strangeways in 1979 as 'four weeks of bitter, racist abuse from National Front screws...Needless to say they gloried in their bigotry by openly wearing their NF badges while on duty. These screws vented their hatred on Irish and black prisoners, especially.'[1]

Following the death of Orville Blackwood in Broadmoor 'Special Hospital' in 1991, an internal inquiry report described the POA members who staff the 'hospital' as a 'closed, in-bred, community of nurses, some from a military-type background, [which] has little understanding of the needs and cultural differences of ethnic minority patients.'

A Home Office Report on prison officers published in 1985 found: 'a remarkably homogeneous group of people. The great majority are middle-aged family men...The majority share some kind of military background in an age where such a background is becoming increasingly rare. They have the kind of educational and previous employment background usually associated with manual workers — but few other social characteristics that would place them as members of the working class community.'[2]

To become a prison officer was at the time of the Strangeways protest, and still is, to join a macho, militaristic culture. Set in its ways, resistant to change: be it the Fresh Start agreement in 1988-9 which restructured working hours (putting an end to the vast overtime payments prison officers had previously been earning) or the integration

1. *Inside an English jail* — Ray McLaughlin.
2. Quoted in *Bricks of Shame* — Vivien Stern.

of female officers into men's prisons. And jingoistic: following David Waddington's visit to the wrecked gaol, one of the first things he did was reassure the POA that Strangeways would be rebuilt. Their response was to sing 'Land of Hope and Glory' in the prison officers' club!

The Press and the POA – a lie repeated often enough...

In October 1985 Broadwater Farm Estate in North London erupted in anger following months of heavy police intimidation and brutality which had culminated in the death of a local woman, Cynthia Jarrett. In the uprising which followed Mrs Jarrett's death, a policeman was killed and all the national newspapers carried accounts of how his head was hacked off and put on a pole. PC Blakelock was indeed killed, but the 'head-on-a-pole' story was completely untrue and many of the papers later said so. Yet the image remained and stained the majority of the public's perception of the uprising.

So too with the '20 dead', '30 dead', 'Castrated, beaten and strung up'-type headlines about Strangeways. They were fiction, complete fiction, for the most part invented by prison officers and police officers and repeated to an eager, receptive audience of blood-hungry journalists. Throughout the 25 days of the siege the 'official' voice of the Home Office press department gave little information and, when challenged, retreated to a 'cannot confirm or deny' position. The POA, fighting its own corner – 'the cause of the riot is understaffing' – shared none of this reticence. Its official spokesmen were everywhere and its unofficial voices whispered in many ears. Manchester POA Branch Chair Ivor Serle gave frequent press briefings in which he repeated his 'gut feeling' that bodies would be found inside, variously citing firemen who had seen them and prisoners who had apparently 'shouted over the wall' that there *were* bodies. The press believed Ivor Serle's guts because his guts rumbled out the words they wanted to hear.

The Press Council's last act before disbanding itself in January 1991 was to produce a comprehensive report into the reporting of the events at Strangeways. It was clear, the report stated, that, 'many of the more gruesome events reported in the press had not occurred – nobody had been systematically mutilated, there had been no castrations, no bodies had been chopped up and flushed down the sewers. Though there was inter-prisoner violence in the first hours of the riot, torture on the scale suggested by many of the early reports did not take place. If mock trials did take place – kangaroo courts, as some papers described them — they did not result in hangings or other types of execution.'

The report found that press coverage 'fell into the serious ethical error of presenting speculation and unconfirmed reports as fact.'

A clear example of how little substance there was in the early press stories is the *Daily Mirror*'s 3 April front page: 'Prison Mob "Hang Cop"' about the apparent execution of former policeman, Dennis Davies, who was serving time for rape. Davies was not even in Strangeways but alive and untouched in Armley gaol in Leeds. The *Mirror* was forced to publish a retraction admitting that its 'reliable police sources' had got it wrong!

But the sickest thing of all is that even after it was quite certain that there were no dead bodies, representatives of the POA kept on spinning the lie. A *Manchester Evening News* reporter told the Press Council inquiry:

'I arrived at the prison on 2 April...I spoke to...Ivor Serle, POA branch chairman, who said that no bodies had yet been found but "I fear the worst"...

'Interesting — and I still have this on tape — Ivor Serle said on 26 April, the day after the siege ended: "I have not yet seen the inside of the prison. I have not been there. Our teams will be going in today to make sure it is safe, to make sure there are no bodies lying around. Then the forensic people will go in and then the structural engineers will go in."'

In May 1990, at the POA conference, Manchester Branch Secretary Peter Hancox had still only very slightly changed the story: 'We are talking about part-castrations, about having to take ropes from around people's necks...We are talking about people bleeding from every orifice of their body, having to run the gauntlet of bricks, coping stones and tiles...They were not animals on the roof because animals wouldn't have done that to their own.'

AIDS horror needles sex shock

Towards the end of the 25 days, when the tabloids were running out of new ways to rearrange the words 'Scum', 'Riot', 'Jail' and 'Horror' and the death stories had finally run their course, some enterprising hacks began to find new ways to smear the protesters. Among these was the *Daily Star*'s 'Rioters have AIDS' and the *Manchester*

The press compound outside Strangeways

Evening News' story that deadly 'Aids traps' had been laid for the prison officers who would eventually retake the gaol. This 'lethal needle plot' consisted of booby traps constructed out of scaffolding poles tipped with needles contaminated with HIV, hepatitis B and 'other viruses'. The source of these stories appears to be, once again, the POA, whose members apparently genuinely believed they would be at risk from such traps when they re-entered the prison.

The *Manchester Evening News* also carried a story about a series of demands Alan Lord had made for improvements in conditions for life sentence prisoners. These included private conjugal or family visits, a right in most Scandinavian and Dutch prisons and some US and Canadian penitentiaries. The *Manchester Evening News* translated the demand as 'Strangeways prison riot leader, Alan Lord, says he will surrender – if he is allowed sex romps in his cell'.

The 'quality' papers

When the siege was over, the tabloid press exploded into paroxysms of the usual filth. But the 'quality' papers were, in their own way, no better:

'Now that the siege of Strangeways has come to an end we can begin to count the many and varied costs of this most disgraceful and unwelcome episode in our national life...A degrading public spectacle has been allowed to develop in a way clearly damaging to the good name of the country...People all over the world have seen television and news pictures showing scenes from Manchester and elsewhere, often portrayed as representing "life in Britain today". At home we have been subjected to the appearance of authority set at nought...The costs of Strangeways have been formidable and will be far-reaching.' *The Daily Telegraph 26 April 1990.*

And it was not just the traditional Tory broadsheets which expressed such sentiments. *The Independent* mustered far more contempt for the prisoners than the *Telegraph*:

'The inmates' occupation of Strangeways prison was nasty, brutish and far too long...These were violent and unstable criminals enjoying an orgy of destruction...[they] were not in the business of rational protest...The prolonged and bizarre nature of this very public siege had two unfortunate side effects. It encouraged copycat riots and it made the forces of law and order look ridiculous....' *The Independent 26 April 1990.*

And *The Guardian* worried that the men who had brought the disgusting conditions in Britain's gaols to public attention had not gone about it politely enough and urged ministers to institute reforms, in order to avoid future embarrassment:

> 'Initially, the riot appeared to increase public support for radical reform of the present degrading penal system. Some of that goodwill will have been eroded by the antics of the rioters in the last two weeks, and may be further eroded once further details emerge during the forthcoming criminal prosecutions. But this must not deflect Home Office ministers from the road down which they had belatedly begun to travel. A change in prison conditions is crucial if good order is to be restored to the system.' *The Guardian 26 April 1990.*

The Guardian's view became, for a while, the prevalent one. The prisoners who had rioted should be punished but prison conditions ought to be improved, not as a reward or a concession, but essentially as a deterrent. By 1992 leading members of penal reform groups were saying privately that they no longer had any differences with the government's position and had entered a cosy partnership in which 'reform' was top of the agenda. Meanwhile, those who had first demanded the reforms were being sentenced to between four and 13 years more imprisonment. And, on this, the press had precious little to say.

When the murder charge against five protesters was dropped half way through their trial in 1992 it was wonderful news for the prisoners and their supporters – but did anybody know about it? No banner headlines screamed 'Strangeways protesters innocent!' 'Final murder count – zero!' The press, both tabloid and broadsheet, was silent. The journalists who gave us '20 dead', '30 dead', 'sex-offenders emasculated and thrown over landings' had nothing to say. The same journalists who heralded the start of the trial with quotes from prosecution witnesses who feared the 'wild animals' in the dock would kill them in their orgy of violence, had been struck dumb. Suddenly the wild animals were no longer wild, the murderers and torturers were innocent and it wasn't 'news' any more.

Chapter Twelve

Solidarity

From day one of the Strangeways protest a presence of solidarity was maintained outside the prison by families, friends and supporters of the prisoners. It was a source of constant irritation to the Prison Service and prison officers and a great comfort to the men on the roof.

The prisoners' families[1]

Sandra Williams is Mark Williams' mother. Prior to the riot she had noticed a deterioration in her son when she visited him in Strangeways. He did not recognise her, was covered in boils and became very thin. She phoned the prison every day and once when Mark was in the prison hospital she spoke to the Medical Officer: 'He called himself a psychiatrist and in his opinion there was nothing wrong with Mark'. It was fellow prisoners who realised Mark was being drugged with largactyl, the 'liquid cosh'. Mark told his mother how on two occasions 'five officers sat on him and injected the drug into his behind...' Sandra noticed that during the protest, when Mark was on the roof, the effects of the drugs wore off and he felt much better. An end to the use of the 'liquid cosh' was one of the main demands of the protest. Sandra Williams supported Mark and the others wholeheartedly: 'they were fighting against the brutality, the conditions and for the Common People... Mark made a stand for his rights.'

Eunice Lord is Alan Lord's sister: 'The response of the press made me really angry.

1. This section is reproduced from interviews with relatives of prisoners published in *Fight Racism! Fight Imperialism!* 95 June/July 1990.

You know the person, you know they're a human being. Those people have never been in gaol. They never put that Alan's in the *Guiness Book of Records* for weight-lifting or the work he's done with paraplegic children, helping them to exercise. Alan and the other prisoners, they're not evil or scum, they're fighting for their rights, like anyone else would.'

Eunice first knew Alan was on the roof after the protest had been going a week: 'I saw him on the TV... I went straight down there. Alan spotted me and told me to go up the side road to talk to him. At first I wanted him to come down, he had too much to lose – he's the only one doing life and I was worried. But after hearing why he was there, I was all for him.'

When Darren Jones' mother, Shireen, heard press reports that a 17-year-old remand prisoner had been hanged in the gaol, she couldn't sleep. She said: 'I was actually thinking of Darren in the past tense... I was grieving for him and believed he was dead... It's the press who are scum. They are not interested in any good points or the truth. All they want is sensationalism and scandal...'

Many of the relatives wanted the siege to end because they were concerned for the prisoners' safety. 'We supported the cause, we were just worried about the consequences...the lads made a stand and were willing to pay for it with their liberty...if they had not done it, bad conditions in Strangeways would have gone on for another 100 years...'

'I've had support from other prisoners, phone calls and letters. Strangers have stopped me in the street, old ladies asking how I am and how's Darren, hoping he's OK. I've not come across one person who's slagged me...'

'I didn't care what any of the lads had done. They were all our boys on the roof, not just my son... if Darren was down and I couldn't see him, it was great to see that Mark was OK... They used to shout down "Eunice, we love you!" and "Mrs Jones, we love you!" And even if we didn't know them from Adam, we'd shout back, "We love you. Good night, lads." They were great.'

'I'm proud of my boy and all of them that took part in that demonstration. We, the families, have got a bond between us that will last a life-time...I'm disgusted at the authorities... the lads had to make a stand themselves against the conditions to get noticed... They'll go down in history like the suffragettes did. They made a stand like women had to for their rights. These boys have done it for prisoners' rights; not just theirs but every prisoner in the country, future prisoners and past.'

The Strangeways siege
by Eric Allison

Looking back now, I realise I had a strong sense of envy towards those lads on the roof. Not in any malicious sense, but an absolute longing to change places with one of them, any of them. I must have felt guilt as well, and shame that I and other previous generations of prisoners in Strangeways had not had the courage to do what those lads were doing now. I was determined therefore to do *something*. I would tell people, as many as I could, what went on in the Strangeways of this world and I would go down there, as often as I could, to show my support and solidarity.

On the Monday, the second day, I telephoned *The Guardian*. I told them that above all else Strangeways had been a 'screws' nick', that they had run the place, not the governors. They were proud of it as well, taking every opportunity to tell you that it was their nick, their writ that ran. And for me, this made it all the more sweet to see them now, huddled together in groups, mute, disbelieving that they had lost *their* prison.[2]

On that day, and until the end, there was much more order than on the first day – at least outside the gaol. Lines had been drawn; the police, fire brigade, press, had organised their areas. Bury New Road was open to traffic so we, the spectators, could get near to the front of the gaol. We could stand and look and wave and let those lads know that we were with them. We could also, and did, let any screws we saw know that we knew full well the extent of their shame and humiliation.

I spent hours at the scene each day. In the evenings especially, there was something of a party atmosphere. The biggest crowd would be when the pubs closed at night. Strangeways became an after-hours addition to Manchester night-life, especially fulfilling for those revellers who had served time. I put most of my hours in during the day though; I seriously expected the gaol to be stormed and I knew that the screws at least (for there was talk of the SAS going in) wouldn't fancy the roof at night.

Of course, it wasn't all euphoric. At that stage I was seriously concerned that there may have been some truth in the lurid headlines referring to the many dead and was relieved to see and believe the *No dead* banner, displayed by the lads on day two. Knowing the system, I felt sure that, given the opportunity, some of the 'ordinary' cons would have vented their anger and frustration on the Rule 43 prisoners and I

2. *The Guardian* printed Eric Allison's comments the following day headed 'It's a bad nick because it's run by bad screws'.

wept real tears when I heard of the death of Derek White, the man on remand for alleged sex offences. Yet, even at that early stage, a pattern had emerged which made me confident that the main protagonists in the riot would not have taken part in the beatings of the 'nonces'. It was clear that only a relatively small group of men would be bent on staying on the roof for as long as possible. These men would become very high profile and must have known they would. It was inconceivable to me that such men would put themselves so much 'on offer', if they had committed the assaults on vulnerable prisoners. Nothing that I know now, five years on, and with much knowledge of what went on inside Strangeways, has caused me to alter that initial view.

One day, early on, I spoke to a middle-aged man from Hartlepool. He had brought his family down for a day out. He told me that 20 years earlier he had served six weeks in Strangeways for debt. It was the only time he'd been in prison, yet all those years on he had made the long journey, by public transport, to rejoice in the destruction of the place.

On another occasion, I exchanged strong words with the Fire Brigade. I'd been incensed to learn that the previous night they had turned their hoses on the men on the roof. I marched into the caravan they were using as a command post and asked to see the senior officer. I told him I'd always supported the Fire Brigade when it had taken industrial action, but would never do so again. Their job was to put out fires; they had no business whatsoever using their expertise to attack working class men who were rebelling against atrocious conditions and treatment. I later phoned their union headquarters and repeated my complaint. The next day, the Fire Brigade issued a statement in the *Manchester Evening News* saying there had been a misunderstanding and that their men and equipment would not be used to such purpose again. Some other people had also remonstrated with the Firemen, using far less polite language. They told them in no uncertain terms that they should be careful, when attending fires in certain areas of Manchester and Salford.

On the Thursday of the first week the Woolf Inquiry was announced and I wrote to the *Manchester Evening News* urging ex-inmates of Strangeways to contact the Inquiry and tell the truth about the wretched gaol.

Ivor Serle, the Strangeways POA chairman, seemed never to be off the television screen. I remembered him well from my time in the prison. A miserable, mean-spirited man, who constantly opposed what little there was in the way of reform at Strangeways. He constantly spoke of the 'professionalism' of his members and how keen they were to retake 'their' prison. They hadn't shown much 'professionalism' or 'keenness' when they ran away and left it in the first place!

At the end of the first week I had to go away for seven days. When I returned I watched video tapes of the TV coverage of the week I'd missed. One incident stood out; a long piece of footage of two lads surrendering. It was very moving for they were young lads and obviously didn't *want* to come down but were clearly being persuaded to do so by some older men. It showed the camaraderie that existed up there and firmly nailed the lie, put out in some quarters, that some people were being forced to remain on the roof.

On the Monday of the third week I hired a powerful megaphone. My lad and I took it down to the nick. He was to read a prepared script to the lads on the roof. We'd chosen the words carefully; we didn't want him nicked for incitement. It turned out to be good sport. After his first reading a policeman came over and ordered him to stop. I stepped out, from the small crowd that had gathered, and asked the cozzer what the lad had done wrong (without indicating that we were together). He asked me what business it was of mine. I replied I was a citizen of Manchester who had some experience of the law (not untrue!), upon which he sloped off to seek advice. An inspector then appeared and told my lad his behaviour could offend or annoy the onlookers. I asked the onlookers if they had experienced such feelings. They replied no, not in the slightest. It then dawned on the cozzer he was being wound up and he became very hostile. We ended it there; we wouldn't have minded being nicked but there was too much to do. We didn't know whether those on the roof had heard our solidarity message but two of them came over the roof to a position nearer to us and we, the crowd, gave them a good wave, which as always they returned.

A marvellous incident the following day. Three lads had surrendered on the Monday with a bad dose of food poisoning and the 'authorities' were trying to use the threat of illness to end the siege. They warned the remaining protesters that, as their food supply would almost certainly be contaminated by now, they were risking serious illness or even death by remaining. The next morning one of the lads, appeared on the roof, bade the City of Manchester a booming and most healthy sounding 'Good Morning'; then proceeded to eat his breakfast in full view of the cameras. After each mouthful, he put his fingers to his lips after the fashion of a gourmet sending his compliments to the chef. It was pure theatre; Chaplin at his best. Following his meal, he took out a small cigar, rolling it under his nose appreciatively before lighting it. Incredible!

Every day was a bonus. I couldn't believe that with the number of men on the roof being so few now, the Home Office would continue the waiting game. But another week went by, and yet another began, until on that Tuesday Ivor Serle gave a press conference in which he indicated most strongly that 'they' would be going in the next day.

The next morning, I was outside Strangeways very early.

A larger than usual crowd had gathered and among them and the ranks of the press there was an air of expectancy. Around 10.30 we could see the remaining lads together on A wing roof. Shortly afterwards, a screw's head appeared through a hole at the end of A wing, then another. The lads now retreated towards the roof of the chapel. Then we saw more screws; a dozen or so were inside the top of the rotunda roof. They made no attempt to come on to the roof itself, nor did the others at the end of A wing, but it was a clear indication that they had recaptured the whole of the nick, bar the small roof area that the lads still held. The screws at the end of A wing stuck up a notice to the effect that they were back in charge and there were to be 'No visits'. (And those two words were seriously intended as a wind-up. Whenever there is any sort of problem in gaol, the first thing they do is cancel visits. Never mind that people may have travelled hundreds of miles; there's 'no visits'. And often for the flimsiest of 'reasons'.)

Around 11.30 a Home Office official was giving a press conference so I wandered round to the 'press enclosure' – a cordoned-off car park. There were usually two or three cozzers keeping the public out but today there was only one and he was busy on his radio. The hacks were gathered round a man called Gander who was reading a prepared statement. He told us what we already knew, that the prison was theirs bar the space we could see. Some of the assembled hacks then asked him a few, bland in the extreme, questions and he answered in likewise anodyne fashion. So I asked a couple of questions. For ages the press had been running stories about 'booby traps' the prisoners had set up. They were supposed to have built a petrol-soaked 'pyre', ready to be torched if any assailants came near, secreted needles from syringes among the barricades and even somehow coated these needles with hepatitis B. (Where they were supposed to get such a thing is anybody's guess.) So, I asked whether the 'liberators' had encountered any of these wicked traps. 'Cannot comment', says he. 'Why not?' says I. 'Because its an ongoing situation and the rioters have access to radios.' I persisted: 'If the rioters are confined to the area which you say, and which we can see that they are, then how can your confirmation or denial of the existence of these traps alter the situation?' He had had enough by now: 'Who are you?' he asks. 'A citizen of Manchester,' I reply. 'Well', says he, 'You're not supposed to be in here. You must get your news from the media, like everyone else.' 'Much good that will do me,' I retort, 'when this lot don't ask any proper questions.' 'That's it,' he says, 'Conference over', and off he stalks. Then, would you believe, two or three of the hacks start having a go at me for ruining their press conference! Some conference!

By mid-afternoon there was a huge crowd around the prison. Clearly the news had travelled that this was indeed to be the last day. All of us 'regulars' were there, including a bunch of anarchists, really nice people who never stopped putting their views across even when right under the eyes of the police. I had great respect for the political groups and individuals who had attended the scene, for veteran anarchist activist Ken Keating who like me had berated the Fire Brigade for their complicity in attacking the protesters, for the RCG whose paper I came across for the first time and whose support for the Strangeways prisoners has been second to none. Some of these communists and anarchists put us ex-cons to shame; we should have been there in our tens of thousands.

I missed the very end although I saw it later on TV. I was doing the rounds of the media, the serious element, exhorting them to make it known to the authorities that they wanted to know what would happen to the lads after they came down. I was reasonably confident not much harm would come to them immediately, but there would be reprisals later, I was sure.

The TV news was full of it that night, of course: repeated showings of the descent of the cherry-picker and the defiant lads' salutes. It was highly emotional viewing; those lads looked so small in contrast to the hugeness of the prison behind them, the prison they had taken and held for so long.

Then the BBC interviewed a Strangeways screw, a seemingly benign, caring, middle-aged man who spoke emotionally about the violence towards the Rule 43s. This was Fred Wright, a man widely feared at Strangeways, with a reputation for violence. I knew then that for me, 'Strangeways' wasn't over. I rang the BBC and asked a woman where they got Fred Wright from and why they hadn't asked any ex-prisoners on to the programme. She said the POA had put him up and had no answer to my other question. So, here we were at the end of the biggest disturbance in British penal history, a disturbance that had raised countless questions about the treatment of prisoners, and here was a man who was the epitome of all that was most rotten in the system, allowed to give the totally unchallenged impression that he and his colleagues were caring and concerned. No, Strangeways was not over by a long way...

From some quarters, of course, the prisoners could expect no solidarity at all:

The Labour Party

Robert Litherland, Labour MP for Manchester Central, visited the gaol on 18 April and advised a continuation of the 'waiting game'. Like the rest of the caring, sharing Labour Party, Litherland was quite happy to 'forget' that it was his party which was in government when the Parkhurst, Hull and Gartree protesters were beaten and punished, and that it had presided over the conditions which caused those protests, that it was during Labour's time in office that NF screws openly paraded at Strangeways and that it had never done a single thing to end slopping-out or any of the other indignities it now bemoaned. So Labour happily berated the Tories for the terrible conditions in 'their' gaols. But, just in case anyone dared mistake this new-found compassion for being 'soft on crime', Litherland had already made a few other converse pronouncements along the lines that the prisoners had 'tremendous animal cunning' and had been trained by 'terrorists'; it was 'up to the Home Office to intervene and arrange for the SAS to take over'. Shadow Home Secretary Roy Hattersley had been calling for force to be used against the prisoners since 5 April and if he didn't say so any earlier than that, it was only because he was too busy ranting about how 'severe' and 'exemplary' prison sentences should be handed out to the anti-Poll Tax rioters.

Political solidarity

During the siege the Revolutionary Communist Group organised two solidarity demonstrations outside the prison. The second, on Saturday 21 April, was supported by the Prisoners' League Association and joined by relatives and friends of Domenyk Noonan. Placards bearing demands for prisoners' rights and for no reprisals could be clearly seen by the prisoners on the roof, although the police deliberately used sirens to drown out the prisoners' response.

Although most left wing newspapers covered the uprising, condemning prison conditions and pointing out that it is the working, not ruling class who are in gaol in large numbers, the only group apart from the RCG, to be visibly active at the scene and treat the issue as anything other than an interesting diversion, was Class War.

If solidarity was important for the prisoners during the uprising, it would become ten times more so once it was over and the authorities began to exact their revenge.

RCG/PLA solidarity picket by prisoners' relatives and supporters, 21 April 1990

Part Four

The aftermath

Chapter Thirteen

Reform and retribution

The uprising shook the whole prison system to its core and the ensuing six to nine months were characterised, to a large extent, by the attempts of various parts of the establishment (Ministers, Prison Department, POA, prison reform bodies) to reassert their own agendas. There was no way that the revolt could simply be dismissed out of hand; its impact had been far too great and its after-shocks continued to be felt, both in defiant escape attempts and in a far grimmer way through the suicides of young offenders and remand prisoners, which underlined once again the reasons the protest had occurred in the first place. So, unable to return to 'normal', the different arms of the system fought to make capital out of the situation and to promote their own particular claims above those of the others.

A long hot summer?

On 27 April 1990, just two days after the siege at Strangeways came to an end, the Court of Appeal was forced to free the Winchester Three, two Irish men and one woman imprisoned for allegedly plotting to kill Tom King, Secretary of State for Northern Ireland, as well as 'conspiring with persons unknown to kill persons unknown'. The three were freed when it was accepted that King himself had prejudiced the trial by making a public statement condemning those who exercise the right to silence, just 24 hours after the Winchester Three had done precisely that. There was no direct connection between this event and Strangeways but many prisoners perceived it as another blow struck against the same system and rejoiced. And when the spirit of the failed Long Lartin escape surfaced once again at Wandsworth on 29 June as five prisoners hijacked a mechanical digger and attempted to break through the outer wall of the prison, assisted by the solidarity of 150 others out on exercise at the time, rumours of a 'long hot summer' of protest began to circulate. Such rumours were fuelled by the POA in its own interest.

POA industrial action

Capitalising on the public focus on prisons caused by the uprising, the POA began intensifying its campaign for more working members and more money. Two separate disputes broke out a week after the Strangeways protest ended. One was not directly connected to the North West as it concerned London weighting allowances; the other began when John Bartell, POA Chair, walked out of a meeting in Manchester after three minutes and announced the union was in dispute with management. Bartell told the press: 'Troublesome prisoners are being dispersed throughout the system with no account of problems they cause or staff considerations.' His central demand was for an extra 600 staff.

Full Sutton and Walton POAs immediately voted for industrial action; Walton, already refusing to take Manchester prisoners, now completely refused to take any prisoner from outside its normal catchment area or any prisoners with 'disruptive records'. The management of Full Sutton, a long-term dispersal prison, had scrupulously avoided protests by prisoners throughout April by a combination of lock-downs and shipping out potential 'trouble-makers' to any other gaol which would receive them, including Walton, on repeated lay-downs. The Full Sutton and Walton screws were soon joined by those from Wakefield and within a very short space of time as many as 30 gaols in the country were either in dispute or in the process of balloting for action and the union nationally was organising a ballot.

The combined effects of prisons wrecked by riot and the POA action was a rapid rise in the number of prisoners being held in police cells. By 1 June 1990 there were 1,069 nationally, 690 of them in the North.

There was not, in fact, any long hot summer, not from the prisoners' point of view, anyway. The POA did not give up trying and on 6 October warned of impending 'race riots', an unlikely event despite intense racism in British prisons, as large scale protests over the years have generally been notable for overcoming racial divisions.

The climate was of use to David Waddington, however, who ended his spell as Home Secretary in minor triumph, announcing the Prison Mutiny law at the Autumn Tory Party Conference and two months later, on 9 November, saving the prison budget from the Treasury axe. The threat of 'another Strangeways' was a big factor in staying the Chancellor's hand.

The prisoners

While all this was going on the prisoners who had taken part in the revolt were largely forgotten; their fate having passed into the hands of the police and Crown Prosecution Service (CPS). The only groups to pay any attention to them, other than their own families and friends, were Partners of Prisoners Support (POPS) who organised a press conference for the families of the prisoners on 17 May, the Revolutionary Communist Group (RCG) which held a series of public meetings and pickets in Manchester, London and elsewhere, the Prisoners' League Associations (PLA) and the Anarchist Black Cross. For everyone else, from the Home Office to the Prison Reform Trust, the prisoners were simply a minor irritation. They had put the debate on the agenda but chosen the 'wrong' methods to do so and while the discussion took place, they would be punished. Nobody was prepared to concede that, had they employed the 'right' methods, no one would have listened.

Police station pickets

At a Manchester RCG public meeting on 3 May, entitled *No reprisals! Victory to the prisoners!*, attended also by members of the PLA, it was unanimously agreed to organise protests in support of any of the prisoners from Strangeways victimised by the system and, in particular, to highlight what happened to the seven prisoners who had remained on the roof until the very end.

Domenyk Noonan sent a solidarity message to the meeting:

'The prisoners have fought and won the battle but now the war is next and we should all stand by these men, who have shown courage and determination. Without working class support their efforts will have been worthless... We must picket every court appearance and show the authorities that they cannot punish a man for protesting against conditions that you would be prosecuted for keeping an animal in.'

The first picket after the men came down from the roof of Strangeways was outside the Crescent police station in Salford, where Tony Bush was locked up 23 hours a day. On the eve of the public meeting Tony was dragged away by police officers during the course of a visit. After a successful picket, which coincided with his birthday, Tony was moved to Littleborough where he was held in somewhat better conditions.

The second picket was outside Longsight police station, Manchester, where Paul Taylor was being held. It was from Longsight that the criminal investigation was being conducted.

The police inquiry

By 1 May 1990 the police had already interviewed 900 of the 1,650 prisoners who had been at Strangeways on 1 April and taken statements from the majority of the prison officers present during the 25 days. These officers had not all been from Strangeways; indeed they had been called to Manchester from as far south as Wormwood Scrubs, Cookham Wood, Blundeston, Bristol and Brixton and as far north as Frankland and Durham as well as from Full Sutton, Wakefield, Preston, Lindholme, Liverpool, Hindley, Garth and other northern prisons. Copious statements from both camps continued to be taken over the next five months. Under the procedures of the Police And Criminal Evidence Act the interviews were tape-recorded and this no doubt prevented some of the worst types of physical intimidation which might have gone on otherwise; it did not, however, prevent a high level of trickery and coercion being used by the police. The following is an extract from an interview conducted at Stalybridge police station on 27 April 1990. DC Elder and DC Styring of Manchester Serious Crime Squad are asking Mark Petrie, aged 19, about what happened in the chapel:

DC S   Was Spencer first up with a stick in either hand, hop-stepping over the benches?

Petrie Yeah.

DC S   Don't be frightened to tell us these things because these are things we know already. They're well documented.

DC E   We just want you to tell us your version of events.

DC S   And I'll tell you why. You know full well now that you were suspected, as I've told you, you're suspected of assaulting.

Petrie I haven't done nowt to no one.

DC S   Right, well.

Petrie   I've told you that.

DC S   Right, we're asking you now for the full picture. Don't be frightened of talking about other people because everyone is talking about everybody, pointing the finger at somebody or other. Somebody's pointing the finger at you. Now you may well be involved, you may not be involved, that's what we're here to try to sort out. If you're not involved, tell us what's gone on, divorce yourself from what's gone on and then we can, we can sort it out, we can verify it. It's like a bloody big jigsaw puzzle to us this and eventually we'll know whether or not you've told us the truth.'

Mark Petrie was interviewed for two solid days in this vein; under immense pressure he named three prisoners and described others in detail but each time the police thought he was co-operating fully, he announced he had been lying. Although threatened with charges of assault and wounding, even attempted murder, he stated categorically that he would not give evidence against anyone in court.

Some of those who later stood trial remained entirely silent when questioned: Mark Azzopardi, for example, was interviewed on three occasions and said absolutely nothing other than 'No comment'. Others carefully replied to questions about their own actions. But a number of prisoners did incriminate their fellow inmates, some trying to 'box clever' by setting up additional meetings, feeding the police false evidence and promising to be witnesses for the prosecution in return for either immunity or lighter sentences, apparently hoping that at a later date they would be able to switch sides again and prove police corruption. Obviously the police encouraged such 'assistance', particularly when it concerned evidence about prisoners against whom they, the local police force, held their own grudges. One prisoner maintains that the police, working together with screws, were prepared to trade false evidence against a Category A prisoner for a passage to Ford open prison. These 'informants' subsequently retracted their statements and stood trial, but by then it was too late to undo some of the damage caused.

When one prisoner made a statement to the police naming Paul Taylor as the perpetrator of various criminal offences, Paul's mother Lily rang the police station where the man was held to inquire about it. She was then arrested on charges of conspiring to pervert the course of justice, for which she was later tried and convicted. She was sent to Risley, where Brendan O'Friel had become governor. According to Paul Taylor, O'Friel was the picture of solicitude: 'Mrs Taylor, I know you have had a terrible time,' he said, and days later he had arranged a transfer to an open prison for her.

Inside stories

Not one of the men who had taken part in the uprising in any significant way whatsoever had an easy ride in the period that followed it; today, most of them are still 'marked men'. By September 1990, the 'ring-leaders' had been dispersed around the prison system: Paul Taylor was in Lincoln, Mark Williams in Frankland, John Murray in Liverpool; Glyn Williams and Martin Brian were still being held in police stations four and a half months after the end of the revolt. Here we describe the experiences of three prisoners who were involved in the protest, in the months after the siege ended.

The remand prisoner – David Bowen

The first of those later convicted for involvement in the uprising at Strangeways to appear in court was David Bowen. On 21 May 1990 he and Yuri Harewood appeared at Manchester City Magistrates' Court, were charged with 'riot by threatening or using unlawful violence' and remanded in custody for a week. Both were remand prisoners at the time of the protest and had since been released. David Bowen would be remanded and released several times, not to mention escaping, before being sentenced to nine years' imprisonment in 1993 and a further three in 1994. David is adamant that his only role in the riot was that of a spectator, a contention not disproved by any of the photographic evidence gathered for his trial.

Not long after David was released on bail in May 1990, he was arrested again for shop-lifting, remanded in custody, sentenced to 12 months' imprisonment, most of which he had already done on remand, and sent to Preston prison to serve the last seven weeks.

At Preston there were a lot of staff from Manchester, which was 'closed until further notice'. They soon realised that David was on bail for the riot and began harassing him with 'silly nickings that lost me some four months in remission... I was kept in the Seg under Rule 43b Good Order And Discipline (GOAD). I'd served 13 previous prison sentences and never lost more than seven days in total or been on GOAD before!'

David was told that if he agreed to move to another gaol for the final three and a half weeks of his sentence, he could come out of segregation and spend the time on 'normal location'. He agreed and was sent 200 miles south to Dorchester prison.

There he received a letter from his solicitor telling him Preston staff had alleged he planned to leave the country as soon as he was released and the Crown Prosecution Service (CPS) was therefore asking for his bail on the riot charge to be revoked.

At the subsequent court hearing David produced the April/May 1991 issue of *Fight Racism! Fight Imperialism!*, which contained a letter he had sent from Preston, encouraging the idea of a protest march at the start of the first trial of the 'rioters'. He said that this, rather than any threat to leave the country, was why the Preston screws were so keen to stop him getting out on bail. David went on to prove that a memo written by a Preston screw, who alleged David had boasted to him about how he would leave the country, had been written at a much later date than claimed and backdated. The hearing took all day, but due to the blatant perjury of the Preston officer, the judge was forced to find in David's favour and renew his bail.

David was released soon after, went to the USA and came back again. He sent Preston prison a postcard from the airport while he waited for his flight home. They took it as an indication he had in fact skipped bail and rang the CPS. It would be an understatement to say that by this time David was not a popular man among prison staff in the North West of England. During the course of his trial in 1992, he escaped, following a series of threats by Hull prison officers that their colleagues at Preston were 'waiting for him' and had 'sent their love'.

As this book goes to press, David is in Walton gaol, Liverpool, awaiting his third trial in connection with the Strangeways revolt, for the escape, and appeal hearings against his convictions for conspiracy to commit GBH and to pervert the course of justice.

The lifer – Alan Lord

On 10 June 1990, the day before the Woolf Inquiry opened, Alan Lord acutely embarrassed both the Prison Service and Manchester police by escaping from custody. He walked calmly out of 'high-security' Astley Bridge police station while the officers on duty watched the World Cup on TV. He was recaptured five days later and imprisoned in Wakefield prison's infamous F wing segregation unit.[1] From here he wrote to *Fight Racism! Fight Imperialism!* that since his recapture he had been placed on the Category A

---

1. F wing of Wakefield Prison was the location of one of two Special Control Units, opened in 1974 to break the will of 'subversive' prisoners. In 1975, after a public outcry, they were officially closed, meaning in practice that the 'behaviour modification' regime was discontinued while the use of the same cells, designed for the purpose of sensory deprivation, continued.

list. Clearly this was a punishment for the embarrassment his escape had caused. He wrote: 'I harmed no one and committed no crime'.

Alan described how police at Astley Bridge had left the keys in his cell: 'I had them five weeks! On apprehending me, the police used unnecessary force. Every one was carrying a sledgehammer etc. Ah well, at least those relatively tranquil days of freedom are memorable.'

On 11 August 1990 members and supporters of the RCG held a picket of Wakefield prison to protest at the conditions under which Alan was being held in F wing: in solitary confinement in a cell within a cell with no window or adequate ventilation.

After five weeks, the light in Alan's cell was left on all night, seriously disrupting his sleep. The first time it happened Alan wrapped his shirt around the light and for this was put 'on report'. He then was forced to sleep under his bed to minimise the ill-effects to his health.

Mark Stoner-Seed, who was in Wakefield at the time, wrote in a letter to *Fight Racism! Fight Imperialism!*: 'The only good thing to come out of my recent spell in the block was that I was able to have a brief chat with Alan who like me got a bit of a buzz listening to the sounds from the demo outside the gate at the weekend. Nice one!'

Alan Lord is still being victimised for his part in the Strangeways uprising. A Category B life-sentence prisoner in 1990, who had served ten years and could have reasonably expected to be decategorised to C in a few years' time and be walking free in 1995-6, he is currently serving 11½ years concurrent with his life sentence, and has little chance of release this century. The life sentence is a wonderful weapon for the system, which can literally expand and contract it as it sees fit. Life for Private Thain, a British soldier found guilty in December 1984 of a shoot-to-kill murder in the North of Ireland, meant two and a half years' imprisonment; for Alan Lord, it could mean life. Furthermore, Alan is now categorised as 'Double A high-risk' and as a result all his visitors are heavily vetted. While researching this book, we applied to visit Alan; the Prison Service refused permission.

Death in Hindley – Iain McKinlay

After his surrender, Iain McKinlay was transferred to Hindley remand centre near Wigan and held in solitary confinement. He was 18 years old. Prison officers at Hindley knew exactly who he was and went out of their way to victimise him even more than was already normal at Hindley. On 24 June, after 49 days of this treatment he wrote a note to his parents and girlfriend and hanged himself.

Hindley had an atrocious record. Between April and August 1990 there were 24 recorded attempts at suicide, including six in one weekend. In February 18-year-old Jonathan Curry had succeeded in taking his own life. On the night Iain killed himself, Anthony Hook, who was in the adjoining cell, did so as well.

Iain's parents were treated appallingly. His father was shown his son's suicide note and asked to identify the handwriting but not permitted to keep the note or have access to any of his son's property until after the inquest, for which no date was given.

When the joint inquest into Iain McKinlay and Anthony Hook's deaths was held in January 1991, the jury heard evidence from former Hindley prisoners, who described how Iain had been subjected to a hate campaign by prison officers who spread rumours he was a 'nonce' and on one occasion put a razor blade in his food. Iain became so terrified that he refused to come out of his cell at all and at one point went on hunger-strike for four days. He wrote a letter to the governor requesting a transfer to a different gaol because he believed his life was in danger from other prisoners, who were being wound up by staff to attack him. His suicide note read: 'I am committing suicide because there are members of staff letting the other lads get on my case'. Although all prisons are issued with guidelines on suicide prevention and supposed to assess prisoners on reception for potential risk, no assessment was ever made in Iain's case. Both Iain's girlfriend and a Salvation Army representative had warned the prison authorities that Iain had expressed suicidal feelings but no notice was taken of the warnings.

After nine days of evidence, the inquest jury decided that Anthony Hook had killed

himself 'in circumstances brought about by lack of proper care' but returned an ordinary verdict of suicide on Iain McKinlay. Tim Owen, the barrister representing the families at the inquest, accused Alfred Jennings, Hindley's governor, of 'appalling neglect' and suggested that the governor would not treat a dog in the way Iain had been treated. Jennings responded with the pathetic excuse that Iain had been kept in segregation for fear he would incite another riot. Even if this were true and one wayward teenager could destabilise the whole establishment to such a degree, it does not explain the bullying or the razor-blade.

The retribution continues

Five years after the uprising, the prisoners convicted of participation are serving their time in the harshest conditions British prisons can offer them. Permanently labelled as 'subversives' or 'trouble-makers', they are subjected to continual harassment, usually in the form of sudden and arbitrary moves from one gaol to another, often involving journeys of hundreds of miles.

As this book goes to press at the start of 1995, Tony Bush, John Murray and Barry Morton are in punishment blocks around the country. They spent Christmas 1994 in prisons on the Isle of Wight, Stockton-on-Tees and Lincoln respectively, far from their families in Liverpool and Manchester. Alan Lord is still one of just half a dozen prisoners isolated in the Special Unit at Hull. Having spent some time back in the prison system, mostly at Wakefield, Mark Williams is now once again a 'patient' of the Ashworth 'Special Hospital'. At Walton gaol in Liverpool where David Bowen has spent most of the past year, conditions are akin to the pre-riot Strangeways.

Barry Morton was moved to Lincoln prison from Full Sutton in York at the end of November 1994 with no warning and no reason given, with just the clothes he stood up in. His property – letters, photographs, clothes etc – remained at Full Sutton. Four days before Barry's arrival at Lincoln, Tony Bush had been moved on from there to Parkhurst on the Isle of Wight, having arrived in exactly the same way as Barry, just three weeks earlier. This is just one example among many: the Strangeways protesters have joined the list of 'subversive prisoners' who are constantly subjected to such treatment. The 'ghost train' is deliberately designed to destroy prisoners' relations with their family and friends by rendering visits and other forms of communication increasingly difficult. It is also an attempt to break their will to fight back by creating constant feelings of disorientation and insecurity.

Chapter Fourteen

The Woolf Inquiry

by Eric Allison

Soon after the appointment of Lord Justice Woolf to head the Inquiry into the disturbances, he announced that the inquiry would not be restricted to the immediate events
but would also deal with their underlying causes.

Of course it was the actions of the prisoners which forced an inquiry of this
unprecedented scope. Immediately the Home Office began to worry that Woolf might
shine too bright a light into the darkest corners of the prison system.

The Woolf Inquiry opened on 11 June 1990 at the Freemasons' Hall in Manchester.
Its first five-week session was an investigation into the events at Strangeways and heard
evidence from 70 witnesses. Every category of prison officer and administrator up to
Brian Emes, Deputy Director General of the Prison Service, was cross-examined.
Conspicuous by its absence was the evidence of the men on the roof. The prisoners
who so vividly dominated our TV screens for 25 days were nowhere to be seen or
heard. When challenged, Woolf assured the public that the 'ringleaders' had been
interviewed in private but would not be appearing at the public hearing in order not to
prejudice future prosecutions against them, to deny access to 'self-publicity' and,
most absurdly of all, because, as the prisoners made allegations of brutality which the
prison officers denied, the Inquiry would become 'bogged down if it tried to establish
the truth'.

The Manchester session

When the Inquiry was announced I had written to the team who were organising it,
giving details of my experience at Strangeways and asking to be allowed to give evidence. I did not receive a reply for some weeks, so I wrote again and telephoned. I

eventually received a letter from the Treasury Solicitor's office telling me that, as my experience of Strangeways was not recent, I would not be required. I wrote a scathing letter to *The Guardian* which they published. I was then contacted by the inquiry team and asked to attend two of the five public seminars which were to form Part II of the Inquiry.

That first day at Manchester was taken up by Woolf explaining his terms of reference and building experts explaining the structural details of Strangeways gaol.

I was very disappointed at the turn-out: a dozen journalists and a dozen spectators. I had absolutely assumed that those groups who purport to campaign for prison reform would be there: NACRO, the Howard League, the Prison Reform Trust (PRT). That afternoon I rang the three organisations who all gave the same answer: they didn't have the resources to monitor such a long inquiry. In the case of the PRT, the excuse may be justified, but surely not the Howard League, and most certainly not NACRO which has hundreds of workers and which was the least apologetic.

The Inquiry team consisted of Woolf, three 'lay assessors' – Mary Tuck, Gordon Lakes and Rod Morgan – and John Lyon, clerk to the Inquiry. Tuck was an ex-researcher for the Home Office but on the liberal side; Lakes an ex-Deputy Director General of the Prison Service and Rod Morgan is Dean of the Law Faculty at Bristol University. He had resigned from the Board of Visitors at Pucklechurch in protest at what he saw was wrong with the system and has spoken out on behalf of justice and fair treatment for prisoners. He assisted me in finding my way through the maze of the Inquiry and later helped me with research for this book.

Then there were the barristers, eight in all, and plenty of solicitors. There was a QC for the inquiry, a QC and a junior representing the Prison Service, a QC and a junior for the Prison Governors' Association, two non-Silks for the Prison Officers' Association, and a barrister for the Crown Prosecution Service, who was mainly there to watch. Counsel to spare, in fact, for all of the vested interest groups except one, the one in the most trouble: the prisoners. 'Where was the counsel for the prisoners?' I was to ask again and again, only to be told that David Latham QC, counsel for the Inquiry, was there for the prisoners, because it was his job to establish the truth. But how could he? He wasn't briefed. They were, all the others; armies of people sat behind their barristers, passing them notes, conferring with them before they asked a question: civil servants, prison governors, POA officials, all briefing their briefs. And not a soul to brief Latham on behalf of the prisoners.

The witnesses

Noel Proctor, prison chaplain, was the first to give evidence about the riot. I expected the worst. Proctor had been at Strangeways since 1979; before that Wandsworth and Dartmoor; all were well known as 'screws' nicks' and Proctor was a screws' chaplain. As described in Chapter 7, Proctor has never spoken out against either conditions or the actions of the screws at Strangeways. He must have seen hundreds of inmates who have been beaten; it is part of his job to go down to D1, the block, where he will have seen men beaten black and blue, men cowering naked in a corner of a strip cell, men in obscene body-belts, lying stinking in their own urine and excreta. But Proctor only speaks about god and the screws and how good they both are. He did not change his tune for the Woolf Inquiry.

Proctor was asked about the atmosphere on D1. 'There were no problems on D1,' he said, 'there were no complaints.' I couldn't believe my ears. The block in Strangeways was a mass of problems and complaints, a huge festering sore, a prison within a prison where men could be abused and the perpetrators be confident their crimes would not come to light. But, of course, none of the learned barristers representing all the vested interests bar one, challenged this blatant lie.

Proctor went from bad to worse: 'The thing that impressed me most [about the riot] was the professionalism of the staff.' 'All the prisoners who came down [from the roof] had been treated very well by the staff.' 'The staff acted with such dignity, they did not allow their feelings to overpower them.' (Really? Were these the same screws who were seen on TV banging their shields and shouting 'Beast, beast.'?) Again none of this was remotely challenged.

The evidence from prison staff

After Proctor, the screws started telling their tales. And I gradually became convinced something was going on that the Inquiry was failing to pick up; namely, either by incredible negligence or something more sinister, some screws at Manchester had actually helped the disturbance take place.

My first shock came on hearing of the extraordinary amount of warning of trouble that the staff had. The gaol was clearly in a very volatile state prior to the riot. For a local prison there was an unusual mix of inmates. There were men doing long sentences, who had been sent to Strangeways on 'lay-downs'; there were a lot of Scousers – and Manchester staff didn't like Liverpudlians and vice versa – and, above all, for a local gaol, an unusually high number of prisoners who were making it clear they were not happy with the terrible regime. Then there were the actual warnings, dozens of them: grasses from all over the nick were telling screws it was going to go off in the chapel on 1 April. One screw told the Inquiry that 'a lot of inmates' had told him they wouldn't be going to chapel on Sunday because of the impending action.

Warnings went on and on until Saturday night when a grass passed a handwritten note to a night screw, who passed it to the Principal Officer in charge. The note said a riot was to take place in chapel the next morning and masks and PP9s (heavy batteries) were to be used. On Sunday morning several members of the chapel choir refused to go to church. There couldn't have been a screw or inmate who didn't know that trouble was brewing.

Nobody told the governors about all these warnings. The screws who received them would normally have written out a Security Information Report (SIR) but not one did so. Indeed they did nothing they would normally have done. To begin with, the senior staff on duty that weekend did not, as they might have been expected to, prevent 'known trouble-makers' from attending church.

This question of stopping men going to church arose at the Inquiry first, not in relation to 'trouble-makers', but in respect of Rule 43 prisoners. A screw named Duffield gave evidence: together with his senior, Collins, he had been responsible for C1 landing that morning. C1 and part of C2 housed the convicted sex-offenders and other Rule 43 prisoners. Duffield said that a governor grade, Halliday, had come to C1 and told him, 'There was going to be trouble in the chapel'. Halliday advised him to go round the men who had put down to attend chapel and, 'ask them, or state to them, that it would be in their own interests not to go'. Duffield told the Inquiry that 'all but one were quite happy with that'. When questioned by Latham as to what happened to that man, Duffield replied (to laughter) 'Well, we said he wasn't going anyway'.

Not long after this exchange, the Inquiry heard from Principal Officer Zegveldt, the senior uniformed screw on duty. Latham asked him, 'Were there any plans for trying to prevent known troublemakers going to church?' Answer: 'Well, you would have to have a very good case to refuse a man permission to go to church'. Latham: 'I understand that'. (He clearly didn't or he'd have mentioned the earlier account of a man being denied his right to worship.)

Neither Zegveldt nor Palmer, the Principal Officer in charge of security who had been at Strangeways for 18 years and is still there, ordered searches that morning. Zegveldt said, 'It would not have been practical'. Other staff gave evidence that in the

Lord Justice Woolf

past, when a thousand prisoners went to and from workshops each day, they were all searched twice daily; that prisoners were still regularly searched when going to the weekly film (shown in the chapel and which drew a much bigger audience than Proctor's preachings) and that the chapel service had frequently been cancelled when warnings of trouble had been received. This clear deviation between 'standard practice' and the actual routine on 1 April wasn't made prominent in the Woolf Report.

The Inquiry was told that the order to 'evacuate the prison' was given at the very moment when the inmates were starting to barricade themselves inside the chapel, with no possible thought of taking over the whole gaol. No words were spoken between any senior staff about the possibility of containing the disturbance within the chapel. And when Duffield and Collins rang from C1 for instructions, they were told, 'Evacuate your staff'. No mention as to the safety of the vulnerable prisoners who, as staff knew, would be in terrible danger. In the event, Duffield and Collins did evacuate the Rule 43s from C1 — they were among the minute number of staff who did behave 'professionally' that day.

The remand prison

Strangeways remand prison, at that time, consisted of four wings: G, H, I and K, although E4 in the main gaol was used to house Rule 43s on remand. The remand gaol was connected to the main prison by two doors: one on G1 and one on G2 (the latter hardly known to anyone and not used throughout the riot). If the remand screws had barricaded the door on G1, entry would have been virtually impossible. Instead, the door was not even double-locked. The rioters entered the remand prison one and a half hours after the chapel went off. It seems they assumed the staff had ample time to defend the remand wings and therefore they had no chance of liberating the unconvicted prisoners. Woolf himself concluded that, 'If prompt actions had been taken, the remand prison should not have been lost and the Rule 43 prisoners on E4 [of whom Derek White was one] should have been able to have been protected.'

At the end of the Manchester hearings, I was in no doubt as to what had happened. The staff, or some of them, had 'allowed' the disturbance to take place. There had always been friction between staff and management and in the weeks leading up to the riot, there had been disputes and threats of industrial action. It would have suited the POA to have a 'quiet riot', one they could contain, then say to their masters and the public: 'Look at the behaviour of these animals. We need more staff, more money.' But they didn't bargain for the level of hatred that their years of tyranny and oppression had built up among the prisoners. Nor did they reckon on their own cowardice when the chips were down.

Prisoners' evidence

Of the 13 selected and unnamed inmates who were called, seven gave evidence in public. (Presumably the six who spoke in private were informers.) Of that seven, three were members of the choir, three were Rule 43s and there was one other — who described the rioters in the chapel as acting like 'animals'. A well-balanced body of inmate opinion!

One other inmate gave evidence, a lad who spent the whole of his home-leave at the Inquiry and who practically forced them to allow him to speak. He attacked the system to a degree; at one stage he spoke of screws stealing prisoners' food on a daily basis. His evidence was taken after all the press had left for the day and no-one cross-examined him.

Seeing the funny side

The Inquiry was not without its lighter moments: a governor named Frost gave evidence, a huge man weighing about 20 stone; at the time of the riot, he was in charge of the kitchens. Prior to the Fresh Start agreement which turned Chief Officers into governor grades, he had been a 'Chief' and his main grievance about the riot (he was nearly in tears when he spoke about it) was the loss of his Chief's hat and jacket and his book of 'classical menus'. There was an amusing exchange on the subject of 'stew': in their culinary ignorance prisoners complained they were given too much stew; they thought that the turgid mess of spuds and veg with the odd wisp of meat which was served up several times a week was stew. They didn't know that on Monday it was a 'fricasse', on Tuesdays a 'ragout', Wednesdays a 'goulash'; they all thought it was stew.

Then there was the screw Rutson, who went off duty on the Friday before the riot, passing a few remarks with the deputy governor on his way out about the rooftop protest a few days earlier: 'Oh what a pair of nuts they were. No support from the other cons. Eeh, its going to be a nice quiet weekend.'

The Taunton session

The second part of the Inquiry was held in Taunton, Somerset and heard evidence about events at Bristol, Dartmoor, Pucklechurch and Cardiff. Taunton went much better for prisoners than Manchester. Latham instructed his junior, Morris, to act directly for the prisoners. Of course, unlike counsel for the Home Office, POA etc, he wasn't briefed. Nonetheless, he cross-examined staff quite vigorously and many admissions were elicited; for example much was made of the fact that staff at Pucklechurch kept the boys who came off the roof in totally bare cells, without clothes, for three days – and they were only boys, remember. A lot of serious allegations of violence were made by several good prisoner witnesses. Some of these lads gave very good evidence indeed and gamely resisted all attempts to rubbish their allegations.

The London seminars

The final stage of the Inquiry was a series of five seminars in London. I attended and spoke at two of the seminars, one on *Active Regimes in Prison* and the last one which discussed the concept of *Justice in Prisons*. (The other three dealt with *Tactical Management of the Prison Population*, *Cooperation with the Criminal Justice System* and *The Administration of the Prison Service*.)

I came away feeling encouraged; it would have been difficult not to, as speaker after speaker urged the Inquiry to do something about the appalling state of our prisons. Indeed there was so much goodwill around the tables that I had to remind myself that some of the participants (Home Office, PGA, POA etc) were responsible for the stinking conditions that prisoners endure daily.

The exercise was not entirely without fault. I made the point that there were only two ex-prisoners at the seminars – myself and Geoff Coggan from the National Prisoners' Movement. I stated that prisoners' voices must be heard and urged Woolf to recommend changes that allowed prisoners to have some form of collective voice. But overall I was forced to take a positive view. The mass of opinion was for reform and Woolf said nothing to indicate that he was in any way out of step with the mood.

I expected many recommendations for change. For example, I was certain Woolf would propose a code of minimum standards which would be legally enforceable. I was hopeful that the Prison Medical Service (PMS) would be brought under the auspices of the NHS. The PMS vigorously opposed it, of course – they are mainly a mixture of quacks and sadists to whom the concept of care means nothing. But the proposal was put forward many times by people of whom I would have expected Woolf to take notice.

During his evidence to the Inquiry, a senior medical officer at Strangeways, Dr Somasunderam, stated that there was a methadone-based drug-withdrawal programme in operation at Strangeways prior to the riot. This was not so. I checked with many ex-prisoners and the organisation Release and was categorically told that methadone had never been prescribed at Strangeways.

At the conclusion of his evidence, this same doctor was asked whether he could point to possible causes of unrest at the gaol. He said that staff morale was low because inmates on disciplinary charges were receiving over-light punishments!

Chapter Fifteen

The Woolf Report

The Report of the Lord Justice Woolf Inquiry: *Prison Disturbances April 1990* was published in February 1991. It was hailed as the most radical appraisal of the prison system this century, a blueprint for the restoration of 'decency and justice into jails where conditions had become intolerable' (*The Guardian* 26 February 1991).

Lord Justice Woolf and his collaborator, Judge Stephen Tumim, the Chief Inspector of Prisons, who joined the Inquiry at the seminar stage, were extremely thorough in procuring material. They sent letters to every prisoner and prison officer in the country, with especial emphasis given to the six 'target' establishments where the most major disturbances took place: Strangeways, Glen Parva, Dartmoor, Cardiff, Bristol and Pucklechurch.

The Report set out to answer four questions:

i)   What happened during the six most serious riots?
ii) Were those riots properly handled?
iii) What were the causes of those riots?
iv) What should be done to prevent riots of this type happening again?

This was Woolf's remit: riot prevention; how to reform the prison system into a smoother-running machine; and how to minimise the possibility of further breakdowns. His Report had similar implications to those of Lord Scarman's 1981 report into the Brixton uprisings. It represented a recognition by an influential section of the ruling class that naked repression was not working and it was time to call in the 'nice policeman'.

The Woolf Report is meticulously compiled and makes fascinating reading. Woolf received 1,300 letters from prisoners and 430 from prison staff and many excerpts are appended to the Report. Predictably, however, the Inquiry gave far more weight to the opinions of prison officers, governors and 'experts' than to those of the prisoners, whose views are often prefaced with qualifying disclaimers. At the five public seminars in London only two ex-prisoners were invited to participate. The Inquiry did make an effort to hold further seminars in prison to meet and discuss with prisoners, but prisoners at Lincoln, where the main prison seminar was held, say that attendance was 'fixed' by prison officers. A similar attempt was made at Long Lartin but prisoners got wind of it and ensured that representatives of their choice attended the discussion, not those handpicked by the staff.

Reflecting the different stages into which the Inquiry was divided, Part I of the Report, *The disturbances in detail*, examines individually the six major riots or disturbances while Part II, *The prevention of disturbances*, is divided into subsections on imprisonment, buildings, management, staff and prisoners, ending with recommendations and proposals.

The Report contains many interesting details. For example, at Strangeways:

'There were six bathhouses for the whole prison. Each bathhouse had 12 showers and one bath (Showers were also available in the gymnasium) . . . Sometimes prisoners had to go without socks or had to wear secondhand shoes which were the wrong size or a shirt without buttons or trousers which were far too large.' *p49, 3.61*

The regime at Dartmoor is castigated and 'drastic action' called for in order to give the establishment its 'last chance'. And the report on Pucklechurch reveals horrific details of the treatment of surrendering prisoners.

The Inquiry made 12 central recommendations which formed a programme for substantial reform of the prison system. The intentions of this reform were made clear:

'The Prison Service must set security, control and justice in prisons at the right level and it must provide the right balance between them. The stability of the prison system depends on the Prison Service doing so.' *p17, 1.148*

The 12 recommendations

'1. Closer co-operation between the different parts of the Criminal Justice System . . .

2. More visible leadership of the Prison Service by a Director General who is . . . publicly answerable for the day to day operations of the Prison Service.

3. Increased delegation of responsibility to Governors of establishments.

4. An enhanced role for prison officers.

5. A 'compact' or 'contract' for each prisoner setting out the prisoner's expectations and responsibilities . . .

6. A national system of Accredited Standards . . .

7. A new Prison Rule that no establishment should hold more prisoners than is provided for in its certified normal level of accommodation, with provisions for Parliament to be informed if exceptionally there is to be a material departure from that rule.

8. . . . access to sanitation for all inmates . . . not later than February 1996.

9. Better prospects for prisoners to maintain their links with families and the community through more visits and home leaves and through being located in community prisons as near to their homes as possible.

10. Division of prisons into small and more manageable and secure units.

11. A separate statement of purpose, separate conditions and generally a lower security categorisation for remand prisoners.

12. Improved standards of justice within prisons, involving the giving of reasons to a prisoner for any decision which materially and adversely affects him, a grievance procedure and disciplinary proceedings which ensure that the Governor deals with most matters under his present powers; relieving Boards of Visitors of their adjudicatory role; and providing for final access to an independent Complaints Adjudicator.' *p433-34, 15.5*

Woolf envisaged a prison system based on small gaols (not more than 400 inmates), divided into units of 50-70 prisoners maximum, where respect and trust could be built up between staff and prisoners. Before and during the Woolf Inquiry many campaigners and prisoners were arguing strongly in favour of a code of legally enforceable minimum standards for prisons, which would define prisoners' basic rights and make them statutory. Woolf did not adopt this suggestion and instead came out in favour of a system of 'accreditation' whereby a series of national standards would be established which prisons would strive towards in order to gain 'accredited status'. The incentives to gain this status were not clear and the standards would not become legally enforceable until they had actually been achieved! Within this scheme, Woolf proposed that each prisoner be given an individual 'contract or compact'. In this arrangement lay the whole crux of his approach:

> 'As an extension of the "contractual" arrangement which we recommend should exist between Ministers and the Prison Service and which already exists between Area Managers and prisons, the prisoner should receive a "compact or contract" from the prison at which he is held . . . .'
>
> 'If the prisoner's expectations were not fulfilled, he would be entitled to enlist the aid of the Board of Visitors or to invoke the grievance procedures to ensure that the prison did not unreasonably depart from the "contract". As a last resort, the "contract" could provide a platform for judicial review. If the prisoner misbehaves then, as a result of disciplinary proceedings, he could be deprived of certain of his expectations under the "contract".' *p23, 1.183/4/5*

Woolf recommended that prisoners be allowed TVs in their cells, that prison officers wear 'less militaristic' uniforms and discard their infamous peaked caps. And there were to be 'incentives' and 'disincentives' towards good and bad behaviour. These were virtually indistinguishable from the old 'privileges' and 'loss of privileges' but appeared to give the prisoner a more active role in deciding whether or not to conform. As was made clear in a section on 'Justice Within Prisons':

> 'It is not possible for the Inquiry to form any judgment on whether the specific grievances of these prisoners were or were not well-founded. What is clear is that the Prison Service failed to *persuade* these prisoners that it was treating them fairly.' *p226, 9.25 (Woolf's emphasis)*

In other words, it is less important that justice is done than that justice is seen to be done. Hence the improved grievance procedure, the independent complaints adjudicator and the recommendation that reasons for decisions previously shrouded in secrecy (transfers, segregation under GOAD, parole knock-backs, etc) be given to the prisoner, 'as soon as is reasonably practicable'.

By these methods Woolf hoped that the discontented majority of prisoners would become contented; that those who would not instigate a protest, but would join one, would be neutralised. All that remained was to deal with the trouble-makers. Here there was nothing new. All the well-worn techniques – Rule 43 GOAD, lay-downs, transfer from a Cat C to a local prison and transfer to a special unit – were examined and although Woolf's advice was that these be 'used sparingly', he did not suggest any significant change. Regarding control of future protests, Woolf unashamedly advocated increased use of water cannon and the continuation of C&R techniques.

One of the most glaring omissions in the Report was that of any commitment to scrap the Prison Medical Service and bring prison hospitals within the NHS. There was a passing reference to a 'full-time medical officer' at Strangeways who 'quite inappropriately suggested that drugs could be used for controlling prisoners when they were no more than a nuisance'. The Report also stated that 'there existed among prisoners a suspicion that largactyl was being used too frequently "down the block" for control reasons rather than medical reasons'. However, no concrete recommendations at all were made for dealing with this nightmare situation.

Nor did the Report in any significant way address the question of the POA. Woolf talked of an 'enhanced role for prison officers' with more training but he chose to place allegations of brutality firmly outside his remit and therefore did not address a crucial area. The protesting prisoners' anger did not arise simply from being cooped up in squalor. Many prisoners, especially young offenders, were being victimised and beaten and were very frightened. The POA, whose members run the gaols in practice, represented a massive block to any radical change. Without their co-operation reforms might be passed but would not be implemented.

The Home Secretary Kenneth Baker responded to the Woolf Report with a commitment to end slopping-out by 1994. He promised a White Paper later that year, (a standard delaying tactic) and announced a list of measures to deal with future protests, including the introduction of a new offence of mutiny, to carry a maximum sentence of ten years. He also accepted Woolf's recommendations for more visits, phonecalls and home leave, and the abolition of routine censorship.

Having embraced the Woolf Report in this way, Baker and the Home Secretaries who succeeded him came under pressure from reformers to implement the Report in its entirety and in the spirit in which it was written. Like his successors, but with more lip-service to the then-prevailing mood of reform and appeasement, Baker did his utmost to resist that pressure. Even the much-vaunted sanitary improvements were delayed and obstructed because of the expense and disruption they caused.

Woolf was no revolutionary; his proposals were designed to contain and control, and to prevent future disturbances but they did set out a basic level of humane treatment. The Report was a disappointment to prisoners and their supporters who were hoping for minimum standards, the abolition of the PMS and measures to curb brutality, but even the implementation of all the improvements which *were* proposed by Woolf would have been a big step forward and an unqualified victory for the Strangeways protesters. It was not to be.

Instead Woolf's Report has been implemented piecemeal, with all the repressive measures finding their way into being and the progressive element being gradually discarded. So, the recommendation that prison overcrowding be made illegal was never taken up but the 'compact/contract' idea has had all notion of redress or review removed and is in the process of implementation, not as a reforming measure but as part of the move towards increased austerity in prison regimes.

Such 'compacts' (the word 'contract' was dropped as it implied legal enforceability) now exist in many gaols, including the reopened Strangeways. They are a cynical way of buying compliance: the prisoner promises to 'behave' in return for being treated with basic human dignity. The most iniquitous clause in the Strangeways compact states that, on the sole word of one prison officer, a prisoner's 'privileges' can be withdrawn for seven days, with no right of appeal.

The whole prison system is currently being restructured along even more overt 'carrot and stick' lines, with Woolf's 'incentives' and 'disincentives' scheme moulded to fit the more repressive mood. In May 1994, the Prison Service announced the introduction of 'coherent systems of incentives, with sanctions, that will encourage better behaviour'. In November 1994, Home Secretary Michael Howard echoed the message, confirming that prisoners would no longer receive 'automatic privileges' but would have to earn by good behaviour a 'core set of privileges', including extra visits, wearing their own clothes, access to private cash and extra time out of cells.

As for Woolf's 'accreditation' system: even this rather vague proposal was never implemented. Instead, in 1994, after endless rounds of 'consultation', during which the Home Secretary vetoed every proposal, the Prison Service settled on its own set of Operating Standards. These standards are not only legally unenforceable, but also riddled with get-out

The 'new' Strangeways

clauses and state clearly on the first page that they 'are not entitlements for prisoners'.

Woolf's suggestion of more visits and home leave was implemented for a while and most prisoners still get more visits than before 1990. However, this looks set to come under attack in the very near future, while home leave is already being savaged. In November 1994, Michael Howard announced a package of measures designed to reduce home leave by at least 40 per cent, including a new offence of 'being unlawfully at large'. There is to be more stringent 'risk assessment', involving consultation of victims and the police. The ground had been steadily prepared over the previous year with sensational reporting of the few cases where prisoners on home leave committed violent crimes. These instances were then carefully fudged with the greater number of prisoners who failed to return from home leave, or who returned late, to produce statistical 'evidence' of mass 'home leave failure'.

To summarise: while Woolf's recommendations fell far short of establishing a firm basis from which prisoners could continue to defend their rights, as a reform programme with a strong control element it was a radical statement; too radical to be implemented by those who commissioned it. But full implementation was never their intention. Even while Kenneth Baker was welcoming the Woolf Report and promising immediate improvements, he resumed the customary tone of disdain as soon as he turned to the subject of the actual prisoners who had prompted the change:

'Nobody should feel that there is an element of "reward" for prisoners in the changes I am bringing forward. There will be no reward for the prisoners that were involved in last year's disgraceful disturbances. Over 40 of them are awaiting trial on serious charges, including murder.

'The events of last April marked a watershed in the history of our Prison Service. We cannot and will not tolerate the savagery and vandalism in our prisons which we saw then.'

This combination of generalised reform and specific retribution set the scene for the trials which took place in 1992.

Chapter Sixteen

The trials

Fifty one men were committed for trial between 13 March and 22 July 1991 on charges of riot, conspiracy to riot, conspiracy to cause grievous bodily harm with intent, conspiracy to commit violent disorder, conspiracy to cause criminal damage and, in six cases, the murder of Derek White. The majority were split into three groups and then charged in various combinations with various offences. Paul Taylor was also individually charged with Assault occasioning Actual Bodily Harm to prison officer Brian McCormack, but this, like the other charges relating to the original protest in the chapel, was not ultimately pursued by the Crown Prosecution Service. The particular charges which the men faced and the precise scope of 'riot' had been carefully considered by the Crown. The year before, the prisoners who were charged with riot following the uprising at Risley Remand Centre[1] had fought a totally political case and won, despite the directions of the judge; this would not be allowed to happen again.

The first trial

Nine men went on trial at Manchester Crown Court on 14 January 1992: Paul Taylor, Alan Lord, 'Tiny' Doran, Martin McLatchie, Nicholas Webb, Andrew Nelson, Jimmy Miller, Brian Parke and John Spencer. They were all charged with riot under Section 1 of the 1986 Public Order Act and the first six were additionally charged with the murder of Derek White. On the first day the Crown dropped the murder charge against Nicholas Webb, aged 23, who was being held in Ashworth 'secure hospital' and could

---

1. See Appendix 2 for full account of the Risley uprising.

hardly walk or talk when he appeared in court. He pleaded guilty to riot and conspiracy to riot. The remaining murder charges were subsequently dropped as well. The hearing lasted until 16 April. Nelson, Lord, McLatchie and Parke were acquitted of all charges but the jury found Paul Taylor, John Spencer, Jimmy Miller and Tiny Doran guilty of riot.

In court

There was a massive security screen around everything to do with the trial: body-searches for the limited number of spectators who were allowed into Court 3; a specially constructed dock with bullet-proof glass sides; and armed police patrolling the precincts of Manchester Crown Square.

All the barristers, solicitors and clerks involved in the trial were obliged to obtain passes and show them every day to inspecting police officers. These police officers were changed every week so they wouldn't get too familiar with the people and not check their passes.

The defendants spent every weekday night for four months in the windowless cells of the Greater Manchester Police Central Detention Centre, situated above the city magistrates' court. At weekends they were moved to various gaols.

Alan Lord's barrister in the first trial was Vera Baird. She describes the way the men were treated:

'There were complaints about the way the defendants were being treated in the "container": it was cold; they weren't being allowed exercise; they were being wound up; screws were playing their radios late at night; the lights were being left on or switched on and off, on and off. A lot of allegations of harassment. It was inconceivable that they could have put up with it, as the trial lasted three months; you could put up with that for a week if you had to, but not three months. It seemed as though they were deliberately trying to get them to kick off in court.'

The prosecution case

The Crown chose to divide the events of 1-25 April 1990 into a series of separate episodes resulting in specific charges. The first trial was to be concerned solely with the events of 1 April on E wing, where Derek White and other Rule 43 prisoners were beaten up. Vera Baird explains how the prosecution presented its case:

'The Crown brought very few prison officer witnesses, maybe two, followed by the chaplain. The majority of the Crown witnesses were prisoners and they put forward as their strongest cards people who were not sex-offenders.

'One witness was called "John" and he gave evidence against Taylor, Spencer, Lord and Nelson. He was serving a sentence for some kind of non-violent dishonesty and said he was a reformed character since meeting Noel Proctor and therefore prepared to stand the pressure of giving evidence! Although he had a good presentation, he was inconsistent. We had an old-style committal and he was cross-examined at committal and was inconsistent between his original statements, committal and trial. Also, he had to leave the witness box for about a week at one point and when he came back he gave different replies to those he'd given a week earlier. It was easy for him to say about the original inconsistencies that he'd been terrified during the riot and remembered better the second time but he couldn't use that now.

'The evidence against Alan was not huge; about four witnesses either described or named him as on the wing beating up Derek White and other sex offenders.'

The murder charge is dropped

'The murder charge came to an end on two bases. Firstly, there was somebody else who looked very like Derek White, who had also been beaten up and who, unlike White, was thrown off the wire. So lots of confusion arose. Even accepting that the witnesses named the right men as doing the beating, they didn't necessarily have the right victim. And secondly, the forensic pathologist had not adequately carried out the post-mortem. There was every prospect that Derek White had died from a pre-existing thrombotic condition.'

The defence case

'As far as Alan's defence was concerned, it was, in effect, alibi: "I was on the roof at the time". And there was a video showing him. Alan's position was that a kick-off happened in the chapel and from there they went out the back way onto the roof. In my summing-up, I described him as like a kid at a party, taking his first free steps for ten years.

'His first thought, when it kicked off, was escape and he came into possession of some keys and set off to escape but realised it was too late; so he tossed the keys away and decided the next best thing was to be out, to go on the roof. By the time he'd got onto the roof, the police helicopter was there. By virtue of the police log and by reference to the doctor, Somasunderam, who saw Derek White when he was brought to the doors of the prison and made a note of what time it was, we could work out that Alan was on the roof before Derek White was injured. So that was his defence.

'The version of the video we had was dreadful and you couldn't recognise Alan. We said we wanted it produced in court but I was saying to Alan, "What's the point?" When it arrived, it was very clear indeed and they apologised for sending us a bad copy! Of course Alan had escapee trousers[2] on and was pretty unmistakable.

'So Alan's defence was alibi and those who identified him on E wing were either mistaken, or deliberately dropped him in it, or were influenced by the publicity into either making it up or misremembering it.'

No politics admissible

'The trouble with this trial was that the kick-off in the chapel was not technically evidence, so Taylor's political speeches in the chapel, for instance, were not considered evidence when he was accused of attacking the nonces on E wing.

'We expected that evidence about conditions would come out under the separate charge of rioting in the chapel but that was dropped. So there was very little in the trial about prison conditions. The strongest testimony was in Paul Taylor's closing speech from the dock. [Paul Taylor began the trial defended by Vera Baird's colleague, Mike Mansfield QC, but during the course of it switched to conducting his own defence.]

'We did put in some information about lifers and the life sentence. We also called character witnesses, even though Alan was a convicted murderer, including a senior officer from Frankland who said Alan had saved his life from attack by a prisoner on a gardening party and a probation officer who said how courteous and appreciative he was.'

---

2. Prisoners considered an 'escape risk' are made to wear 'patches'– trousers and jackets with bright yellow patches.

The sentences

The sentences handed out to those convicted were as heavy as the judge had the power to make them: Paul Taylor was gaoled for ten years, John Spencer for nine and a half (eight years for riot and 18 months for contempt of court), James Miller for seven and Tiny Doran for four. Although acquitted of the riot charges, Andrew Nelson was gaoled for 18 months for contempt of court following an incident in which it was alleged that he and John Spencer threatened the lives of the jury. Paul Taylor would also face a further charge regarding an alleged attempt to influence the jury and be sentenced to an additional three years.

By the end of the first trial the state's costs – refurbishing the prison, the police inquiry and this first of two major trials – had reached £112 million.

The second trial

The second trial opened on 5 October 1992. There were 14 men in court. Having been acquitted in their first trial, Alan Lord and Andrew Nelson had been added on to the list of defendants in the second. Martin Brian and Earl Fahey pleaded guilty to violent disorder and were sentenced to four and five years respectively; following two years in custody on remand, this gave them their freedom. The others pleaded not guilty to conspiracy to commit GBH with intent and conspiracy to riot. David Bowen and Mark Azzopardi, who had been on bail since soon after the protest ended, were now remanded in custody. Various excuses were used to justify this move: in David's case, that as a spectator at the first trial, he had been involved in plotting to influence the jury; in Mark's that he had reoffended while on bail.

Andrew Nelson and Darren Jones were acquitted; the remaining 10 found guilty of conspiracy to commit GBH with intent, the conspiracy to riot charge being posed as an alternative and therefore automatically dropped when guilty verdicts were announced on the first charge. Six men escaped during the course of the trial, one of them twice.

The episode dealt with in this trial was the so-called 'riot on E wing' on 3 April. In the first trial, the victims of the alleged attacks were other prisoners. In this case the supposed GBH was perpetrated against the riot-clad prison officers who tried to retake the gaol.

Again the defendants spent weekday nights in the Central Detention Centre and at weekends were dispersed to various gaols. At many of these, prison officers took their own extra-judicial revenge for the riot. During the second week of the trial, Tony Bush wrote to *Fight Racism! Fight Imperialism!* 'on behalf of 12 innocent men':

'Thank you for your letter of support. I am located in the same cell as John Murray who is unable to reply...the reason for this is that on 2 October John was ghosted from Whitemoor dispersal prison to Armley gaol, Leeds. On arrival John was met by a welcoming committee who assaulted him and damaged his property. They did not realise at first that John was due to appear at Manchester Crown Court for the protest at Strangeways. Whilst he was being assaulted, a principal officer ran into the strip cell and told the screws who were hitting him to stop, as he was on trial on Monday. The screws immediately left...then returned some 10 minutes later with hot food and clothing. They asked John to shower but he refused, stating he was going to leave the blood on his body, face and clothing to show the court. The officers then became aggressive and in the end John was stripped naked and hosed down. He spent his remaining time in the strip cell and was brought to court by Category A transport. On arrival at Manchester he made a complaint to his counsel and also a governor grade who attends court from Monday to Friday.

'By Friday John's facial bruising had begun to subside and he again approached the governor, who stated that John was not seen by her to have any bruising on Monday and therefore there was no reason to fear for his safety at Armley over the weekend. But, as John's solicitor and counsel had seen the injuries on the Monday, Armley now came up with jumped-up charges of assault on John to counter any allegations. A request before the judge was made but it became quite clear that His Honour Judge Sachs is hostile to any application by the defence. John is under constant emotional suffering at the thought of returning to Leeds weekly. His wrists are still numb and he may have to seek specialist examination as to why his hands are still numb some 15 days after excessive force was used by the Control and Restraint screws who nearly broke his wrist and have damaged ligaments and tendons. There is an inquiry by Leeds police regarding this.

'Kevin Gee, who has been beaten in HMP Liverpool's notorious H1, is now being housed at HMP Preston. Kevin was doing quite well at this gaol until it became common knowledge that he was a Strangeways protester. When he returned to Preston after the first week, Kevin was involved in a fight with at least four prison officers. He received severe facial bruising. His counsel have had his injuries photographed and the police at Preston are to be informed. Right on cue,

Kevin is now being charged with assault on a prison officer and is now in isolation. After some six years spent in local gaols, with no family, Kevin was a vulnerable target for reprisals.

'Mark Williams is the most vulnerable prisoner out of all of us. He is in the notorious Ashworth Secure Hospital and is under a heavy screw escort and heavily sedated. Only after threats of dirty protest and aborting appearances in the dock, were we allowed to see Mark. He sat among us and began to break down and cry. It was very moving, as he tried to explain how he has been told directly by POA screws who hide behind white coats, claiming to be nurses, how if Mark gives evidence regarding how he was forcefully injected and had medication hidden in his food, they will make recommendations that an order of ten years will be enforced. Mark is "emotionally vulnerable" and these perverted screws are going for all our weak points to deter us from giving evidence. I could describe dirty tactics used against every one of the 12 of us.'

In court

Eric went to court to watch the trial; at the end of the sixth week he wrote:

'Unlike the first riot trial, armed police are not in evidence but the 12 are in the same bullet-proof dock constructed for "Strangeways One" and relatives and friends of the accused – and members of the public – are subjected to screening and searching before being allowed into the public gallery. As in the first trial, this farce is solely for the benefit of persuading the jury that they are dealing with a dangerous and organised group.

'By Day 30 some 50 out of the 226 witnesses had given evidence. The main feature of contention to date has been the testimony of the screws who were on duty during the riot. In virtually all cases evidence given in court by these men bears little or no relation to the statements they made following the disturbance – both in de-briefing written form to the Home Office and in their initial statements to police. Officers who at that time (April/May 1990) were unable to identify individuals and their actions are now perfectly certain that such and such a man on trial committed such and such offences. The defence are having something of a field day in respect of these sudden (two and a half years after the event) recollections and it has been particularly pleasing to see witnesses positively squirming under cross-examination. They are of course more used to giving evidence in prison adjudications – where the odds are stacked massively in their favour and where their words are usually taken as gospel.'[3]

The cases against all the men were riddled with inaccuracies, some more blatant than others. The case against David Bowen, for example, rested on untenable ID evidence and had him involved in two attacks at different locations at the same time.

Escapes and sentences

On Monday 7 December 1992 David Bowen and Mark Azzopardi escaped from the prison van bringing them from Hull Prison to Manchester Crown Court. Mark Azzopardi later pleaded guilty to escaping and David Bowen not guilty. His defence was duress at the hands of prison officers.

> 'I was on bail for most of the time after the riot. Two years is a long time from charge to trial. I came back from America for it. I wanted the trial and would have been acquitted. But they kicked the fuck out of us, both physically and mentally. We heard stories every Monday morning, after the weekend break in gaols, of how co-accused were kicked about, and they had the bruises to show for it.
>
> 'So when I was attacked myself in Hull prison the night before my escape, I snapped and decided I would crack up if I did not get away from them. I knew if I told the judge about the attack he would do nothing about it.'

On 17 February 1993 Alan Lord, Barry Morton, Tony Bush, John Murray and Mark Azzopardi (who had been recaptured) escaped from the Crown Court Detention Centre. They were all eventually recaptured but when Judge Sachs handed down his sentences, only five of the 12 convicted were in the dock to hear them. David Bowen was still on the run and Mark Williams, who had been mistreated and drugged by the authorities for years, had been taken back to Ashworth Secure Hospital. The sentences were as follows: Alan Lord, Kevin Gee, Glyn Williams – 10 years; Tony Bush, David Bowen – 9 years; Barry Morton, Mark Azzopardi, Mark Williams – 8 years; Nathan Gaynor – 7 years; John Murray – 4 years.

---

3. 'Second trial opens' *Fight Racism! Fight Imperialism!* 110 December 1992/January 1993.

Judge Sachs promoted

The second trial cost £2 million. Judge Sachs told the Strangeways men, when he sentenced them: 'You had your period of arrogance and violence in front of the world, but now the price must be paid and paid by you'. He was promoted to the High Court a few months later; the only former solicitor ever to become a High Court judge. There he has presided over various notable cases including that of alleged 'terrorists', Martin McMonagle and Liam Heffernan in December 1993. Sachs sentenced them to 25 and 23 years imprisonment respectively for 'conspiracy', on the testimony of an MI5 agent, Patrick Daly, who had set up the entire operation they were involved in for the sole purpose of entrapment.

The third trial

There really was no 'Strangeways 3'. After the second trial 26 men were still due to be tried but the state had had its pound of flesh and was offering plea-bargaining in some cases and even dropping all charges in others. Having seen their friends sent down for eight or nine years for relatively minor or, in some cases, no involvement, prospective defendants accepted the deals on offer, pleading guilty to violent disorder (a middle-range Public Order Act charge) in exchange for the dropping of other charges.

John Hughes and Eric Bell were divided off from all other defendants and set down to be tried together for conspiracy to riot. John's charges were dropped in March 1993 when gross inaccuracies were shown up in the prosecution case. He had originally been due to be added onto the group in the first trial, then was told he would appear in the second. By the time the Crown had settled on preparing a separate case against him, it was in the awkward position of reliance on witnesses whose testimony had already been discredited on two previous occasions. From a possible 27 witnesses, the number was reduced to four and the charges then dropped. Eric Bell's trial went ahead in June 1993 in front of Judge Sachs and he was acquitted.

However, state revenge against John Hughes for his visibility during the early part of the protest was still exacted by the 'informal' route. Having been a Category B prisoner on 1 April 1990, when he came off the roof two days later he became Category A and remained 'on the book', as the top Category is described by prisoners (on account of a log book kept by prison staff in which they record the movements of Cat A prisoners around the gaol), for the next three years.

Ian Allen went to court on 20 September 1993; the only remaining defendant to maintain a plea of not guilty. He was convicted on the flimsiest possible identification evidence of conspiracy to commit GBH and sentenced to 30 months in gaol. Four others who had entered guilty pleas received sentences of 12-30 months. Ian, who was 28 at the time of his trial and had spent a total of six months (not all at once) outside gaol since he was 15, was a remand prisoner in April 1990 and left the gaol on the first day. The case against him centred on whether or not, between being let out of his cell by other prisoners and surrendering at 4.30pm, he had gone to the roof and thrown slates at prison officers.

More trials and tribulations

Judicial revenge did not end there: on 18 March 1994 Alan Lord, John Murray, Barry Morton and Tony Bush pleaded guilty to escaping on one occasion and Mark Azzopardi on two. They were sentenced to 18 months' imprisonment each for the escape from Manchester Crown Court and Mark Azzopardi was given a further two years for escaping on the way from Hull prison to court.

Patsy Marsh, a legal clerk at the solicitor's firm representing Tony Bush, pleaded guilty to helping Bush and Lord after their escape and not guilty to helping them plan it. She was tried separately, four months before the men's sentences were passed and acquitted on the second charge but sentenced to a year's imprisonment on the first count.

Then, in July 1994, to the shock of all present, a Manchester jury found David Bowen guilty of conspiring to pervert the course of justice by attempting to influence the jury in the first riot trial. Paul Taylor had already pleaded guilty to the same charge. Both were sentenced to three years' further imprisonment. David is appealing against this and his other conviction.

All but one of the men convicted in the second trial, as well as Paul Taylor and Jimmy Miller, who were convicted in the first, are appealing against either their convictions or the sentences imposed. A joint appeal against sentence, on behalf of nine men, is due to be heard this year.

Chapter Seventeen

Afterword

I

In 1993 we asked three prisoners for their views on the effects that the 1990 uprising had had on the prison system:

Peter Jordan Political prisoner 1984-93 (Risley, Strangeways, Armley, Long Lartin, Full Sutton, Horfield):

The revolt by prisoners against degrading physical conditions and the inhuman and barbaric treatment of prisoners by Strangeways screws gave inspiration to prisoners throughout the system to launch a massive series of protests and uprisings during the whole of that month.

At that time I was in Full Sutton, having been ghosted from Long Lartin due to a complaint I was pursuing against a screw who had interfered with my mail. As my family lived in the South West, I refused to accept the normal visits procedures and involve the family in journeys of hundreds of miles for a relatively brief visit. I saved up my visits allowance under the system known as accumulated visits, which meant I could get a temporary transfer once a year to Horfield Prison in Bristol.

My first accumulated visits period was during Christmas/New Year 1989-90, ie *before* the Strangeways revolt. Horfield may not have the reputation of Strangeways, Armley, Wandsworth, etc for institutionally organised savagery, but my 28 days in the main A wing were a succession of total deprivation of even the minimum of prisoners' rights on the wing, and harassment of me and my family during visits. On my way back to my cell, after one visit, the dog-handler screw escorting me back raised his fist to assault me and was only restrained by the fact that another screw was present and we were in an area where there may have been other witnesses. On a subsequent visit (the last one I was entitled to that time) the same screw had arranged it so that he would be in charge of the visit and when I started to tell my family that this was the man who had threatened to assault me, he terminated the visit.

The following year at Christmas/New Year 1990-91, *after* Strangeways, I again went to Horfield for accumulated visits. The first welcome sight was that of A wing completely gutted and surrounded by scaffolding, still being rebuilt and renovated after the Horfield revolt of 8 April 1990. The next welcome sign was the very different attitude of the screws. Whereas on my first visit they were arrogant and blatantly noisy and aggressive, always threatening and very clearly enjoying themselves in their (imagined) totally dominant position over prisoners, this time it was clear that the experiences of the Horfield, Strangeways, etc uprisings had scared the shit out of the whole prison administration. Naturally, by their very nature, the screws and governors were still an obnoxious crew but it was clear that they were, no doubt very reluctantly, holding back some of their pre-riots arrogance, aggression, viciousness and triumphalism. My accumulated visits period this time, on D wing and in the visits area, left me with more conviction than ever that prisoners, provided they act in unity, can always defeat a prison system which attempts to run on the lines of Strangeways, Armley, Wandsworth, etc.

It is of course inevitable that the state will try to find new methods for the control of prisoners, as is happening in Whitemoor. But the cumulative effects of Strangeways throughout the prison system have been enormous and the fear of a repeat of Strangeways is making most screws think twice before trying out again their previous practice of treating prisoners like caged animals.

David Bowen (on remand at the time of the riot, now sentenced to 12 years):

Strangeways has changed 100 per cent. Reports of TVs, toilets, sinks, single cells or double (as requested), contracts of hours out of cell, work (other than mail-bags), showers when requested, humane staff, clean sheets, clean cells, no stinking buckets... all sounds too good to be true really, but for Strangeways with the media attention which it gained, inevitably change for the better had to take place. Things couldn't have got worse in that gaol. However, while comrades in Manchester will live with a little dignity, those in Durham, Leeds, Hull, Liverpool, Preston, Winchester, in fact all other local gaols in the UK, still have the same system four years after the riots.

Twenty-three hour bang-up still prevails, 'piss buckets and piss-poor attitude' still holds, true to POA standards, in local gaols. Liverpool gets worse with each report and if stories of Whitemoor, a brand new dispersal with a heaven-sent chance to actually start afresh are true or near the truth, it is clear that no lesson has been learned: kick a dog too much and it will turn and bite back. More riots maybe?

I feel the POA and government have learned very little from a riot that shook the world. Maybe it will take another before they are brought to book for doing nothing that Woolf really thought should have been done.

John Bowden (prisoner in English gaols 1980-92, 18 months at large, now a prisoner in Scotland):

Within a prison system that had relied so heavily on brutality and an institutionalised denial of basic human rights, the Strangeways uprising represented an eloquent statement that things would never again be quite the same. The old order was indeed changing and never again would regimes that had existed in gaols like Strangeways prior to the 1990 revolt possess the same potency to terrorise and subdue. Prisoners had shown that even one of the most brutal gaols in England, a true bastion of screw power and authority, could be reduced to a burning wreck if and when prisoners decided that enough was enough.

The lesson was certainly not lost on those who manage and administer the prison system. In addition to and maybe despite the appointment of Lord Justice Woolf to lead the most far-reaching and extensive inquiry ever into the prison system, the official response to Strangeways also included a more clandestine and sinister re-examination of prison regimes and methods of control.

The liberal façade of Woolf was coupled with a hidden agenda motivated by revenge and a determination to eradicate protest on the scale of Strangeways for ever more. The era of the New Generation prison had arrived, symbolised by high-tech coffins like Whitemoor.

And so the struggle of prisoners continues. Strangeways was a high point in that struggle, a magnificent explosion of solidarity and courage, a true revolutionary act that inspired and strengthened prisoners everywhere.

II

Eric Allison:

During the last two years I have visited many of the lads who took part in the uprising; they are serving long sentences in prisons up and down the country. They have a lot in common with one another, apart from being excessively punished for standing up for their right to be treated as human beings. To a man, all those I have seen had spent many years in gaol before the riot and, to a man, many years in 'care' before that. The pain they have suffered and witnessed is mirrored in their eyes and yet their spirit is unbroken.

These men have been made the sole scapegoats for a stinking system and, in the years in gaol that lie ahead of them, there is further abuse to come. No-one else has been punished: not those in the Home Office, who knew all about conditions in places like Strangeways before the riot, nor their political masters, nor the staff who ran away from Strangeways that morning. Not one of these politicians, officials, governors or screws has been so much as officially censured (the same Principal Officer who was in charge of security that weekend is still a PO in charge of security!).

Lord Justice Woolf recognised the validity of the prisoners' grievances: 'The conditions, prior to the riot, were still, so far as the vast majority of inmates were concerned, with justification, regarded as being wholly unacceptable or inhumane...' After Strangeways everybody connected with the prison industry, and even the Tory press, agreed that conditions in British gaols were intolerable. Yet only those whose tolerance ran out were punished.

Now the backlash is in full swing. The improved conditions won as a result of the riot are being attacked from all sides. But those better conditions are not universal within the system. Thousands of prisoners are still being banged up for 20 or so hours a day; they are still pissing or shitting in buckets in the same 8 feet by 12 feet boxes in which they eat and sleep. Prisoners are still suffering gross physical abuse at the hands of uniformed bullies. At Full Sutton, a modern prison, last summer, a mild inoffensive man whose only crime in prison was standing up for his rights, was being 'exercised' in handcuffs, naked and covered in his own excrement.

The prospect for the future is even more depressing: there are plans in progress to open up a dozen or so secure units for offenders between 12 and 14 years of age. These new prisons will process children into hate-filled hardened adults. Do not be surprised when one day *they* say enough is enough.

III

Nicki Jameson:

The Strangeways uprising was the biggest and boldest in British prison history. It made the whole country sit up and take notice. From being a 'non-issue', prisons were suddenly something on which people had views, of all varieties.

The riot brought reform. It brought recognition of prisoners' human rights. It brought vast improvements to the conditions at Strangeways itself and some improvements at all prisons. Where lobbying and petitioning, both by reformers and prisoners, had had almost no effect, direct action succeeded.

But it also brought increased repression. The government and its various agencies have studied their mistakes and learned from them, putting this knowledge to work in various ways: reshaping both prison architecture and regimes, creating new laws; all to lessen the possibility of such resistance happening again.

There has, however, never been any such ambiguity in the treatment meted out to the Strangeways protesters themselves. They were and still are being severely punished for blowing the whistle. None of the reform groups which so welcomed the post-Woolf 'liberalisation' and are now bemoaning its demise have ever seen it as their job to defend these men. That task has been left to us and we are proud to have taken it on.

With more and more asylum-seekers being detained in British gaols, increasing imprisonment for debt and fine default, the continued persecution of Poll Tax non-payers and the draconian powers of the new Criminal Justice Act, the prison population is set to spiral out of control. Already governors, led by former Strangeways governor, Brendan O'Friel, now Chair of the Prison Governors' Association, are demanding that the state hold back on its power to imprison travellers, squatters and demonstrators. Not surprisingly, O'Friel fears the addition of a new generation of more politicised prisoners to an already volatile and overcrowded situation.

It is unlikely that today's Tory government or tomorrow's Labour one will heed O'Friel's voice of experience. More and more young working class people will be herded into British gaols, their crimes no longer only the survival tactics of poverty, but also a more conscious refusal to participate in a society which offers them nothing.

With more and more prisoners and a new round of increased repression within prisons, there will be more protests, more revolts, more uprisings. It is vital therefore that a movement is built now which supports the demands of prisoners and which can defend them when they stand up, as the Strangeways men did in April 1990, and call time on the brutality and the repression. It is a fight for us all.

Appendix One

On Strangeways

Strangeways trial verdict: savage sentences – Eric Allison [1]

The first Strangeways riot trial is over. For those of us unable to attend, news of the proceedings was scarce. The national press, which had given the riot massive coverage, told us only of the lurid horror stories which emerged from the prosecution's opening speech, the verdicts and the sentences. We heard virtually nothing of the defence arguments; nothing of the conditions, and attitudes, which drove the prisoners to start the protest that was to shake the system by its roots and which put the issue of our lousy gaols on to the political agenda. Was the silence of the press part of a move to put prisons back into the wilderness?

We know that the authorities threw a massive security screen around the trial: body-searches for the limited number of spectators who were allowed into Court 3; a specially constructed dock with bullet-proof glass sides and armed police patrolling the precincts of Manchester Crown Square. All designed of course to give the public – and especially the jury – the impression that the defendants were part of a dangerous and organised group; and not simply a number of individuals who had been driven that one step too far by a combination of disgusting conditions and an oppressive regime.

We can only wonder why Mr Justice Mantell took the view that the scale of the riot had been anticipated by those in the dock and that 'The riot had nothing to do with real or imagined grievances.' His much senior colleague, Lord Justice Woolf (after the most exhaustive and far-reaching inquiry in penal history), was of the firm – and

---

1   All the articles in these appendices first appeared in *Fight Racism! Fight Imperialism! See page 181 for details.*

unchallenged by any vested interest – opinion that the disturbance was planned as a limited protest about prison conditions and that those who planned it – and the majority of the inmates – shared the belief that conditions in Strangeways were 'unacceptable and inhumane.' Perhaps His Lordship should have been called as a witness for the defence.

Virtually all the judge's reported remarks on sentencing concerned the violence meted out to the Rule 43s: the 'wretched creatures whose offences placed them at the bottom of the prison scrap heap'. I know full well, from many conversations with fellow inmates over many years, that I will be in a minority when I say that this aspect of the riot saddened me. I am sorry that the majority of cons don't accept that, in playing the 'numbers' game, they are helping their keepers to divide and rule. (If there were no 'beasts' inside, then the screws would invent some – indeed they already do in some malicious cases. They would – and do – try to turn white against black, English against Irish, etc.) I am sorry that they will not accept that alleged sex-offenders, for example, can be fitted up just as easily – and as often, it seems – as alleged terrorists or robbers; that even if they *are* guilty, 'nonces' need treatment – to stop them from *doing* it, apart from anything else. Prisoners should not judge other prisoners; there are many offences that I find distasteful; assuming it were possible, it is not for me to ill-treat those who, allegedly, have committed them. My enemies inside are those who abuse *all* prisoners.

These remarks are not intended as judgements passed on those convicted; nor to detract in any way from my total support for them. In the first place, I do not know if the men convicted of riot were guilty of the assaults. (I do know that the majority of witnesses to the beatings were grasses; and I give an educated guess that their pieces of silver came in the coin of early release.) And secondly, I understand the desire of prisoners to vent their frustration and hatred of the system on *someone*. Furthermore, if the abuse of those wretched creatures was the main reason for the judge's condemnation of the men in the dock – and his remarks indicate that this was so – they should not have stood alone. What about the judges who send vulnerable prisoners to gaol, *knowing* of the treatment they get? What about the Home Office which presides over the system which divides and rules in this way? What about the screws, some of whom inform 'normal' prisoners about the details of other inmates' offences and turn blind eyes to the beatings of 'beasts'? What about the officers on the day at Strangeways who were fleeing the prison in droves, at the same time as the protesters were barricading themselves *inside* the chapel?

'[The prisoners] were almost certainly astonished that they were so successful and that they were able to take control of the whole prison . . . If prompt action had been taken, the Remand Prison should not have been lost and the Rule 43 inmates on E4 should have been able to have been protected.' *p104/7, 3.432.2/16*

The Prison Service is a vital weapon in the armoury of the establishment; Woolf therefore would be bound to mince his words. Those of us who have witnessed and/or felt the brutal actions of the bully boys in Strangeways and other gaols will be more forthcoming; we know that, like all bullies, they are cowards at heart. Why have those who left 'their' prison (and Strangeways was, above all else, a 'screws' nick') in such unseemly haste not been castigated? When they ran, they left those vulnerable prisoners behind them.

What about newspapers such as *The Sun* (the most-read paper in our nicks. Don't its inmate-readers know that *The Sun* headlined the rioters as 'scum'?): should *they* not be charged with incitement when they brand sex-offenders as 'beasts' and 'monsters'? In one report *The Sun* spoke of such men 'getting the kicking they so richly deserve'. And finally, what about the public? How many of them would have wept genuine tears when they heard of the 'nonces' being beaten? Not too many *Sun* readers, that's for sure. No, it is scaling the very summits of hypocrisy and cant that only those in the dock should have received that scathing condemnation from this ignorant judge.

Those convicted got more than condemnation of course. They received savage sentences. They will not have an easy time inside: those in charge of them will not forget how the protesters took control of one of the flagships of the penal fleet; how they humiliated the Prison Service in general and the regime at Strangeways in particular. We, prisoners and ex-prisoners, must not forget these men either. Nor must those who purport to be friends of prisoners disown them – and there has been a marked, and regretful, lack of disapprobation at the sentences from the more established reform groups. We owe the men a massive debt. Without the Strangeways riot there would have been no Woolf Inquiry.

The findings of that inquiry indicated a measure of understanding of the behaviour of those who took to the roof:

'. . . there are three requirements which must be met if the prison system is to be stable: they are security, control and justice. . . sufficient attention has to be paid to each of the requirements [and] they must be kept in balance. . . The April 1990 disturbances were a consequence of the failure of the prison system to conform to these basic rules.' *p225-6, 9.19/21/22*

'As always the people on the receiving end of this power struggle [between the Governor and the POA in Dartmoor] were the prisoners, who saw their regime diminished in a prison where few, if any, of them wanted to be.' *p156, 5.199.1*

They also pointed the way to the government promising to implement a massive programme of reform. The reforms do not go far enough, nor will they come quickly enough; but prisoners who take advantage of the new privileges which do come their way should know *exactly* who to thank for them: in the words of Geoff Coggan (National Prisoners' Movement) in his opening contribution to a Woolf Inquiry seminar,

'I wonder if we can just remind ourselves why we are all here. It is not because somebody on high decided it was about time something was done about the appalling state of our prisons. It is also not because of the many reform groups that are so eloquent around this table – and in that criticism I include ourselves. . . The only reason we are here at all is because serving prisoners at Strangeways had reached the limit of their endurance and decided to blow the whistle.'

The Strangeways five and those that follow (and the men from Dartmoor, Cardiff, Bristol, etc who took part in the April 1990 uprising and who have suffered or will suffer for it) belong to the only 'party' in the penal system to be punished for the exposed and accepted failings of that system. They must not be forgotten.

Strangeways – the new and the old – Eric Allison[2]

Four years after the biggest uprising in the history of the British prison system, the brand new Strangeways prison has begun to take in prisoners.

As part of the drive towards privatisation of the prison system, Strangeways was 'market tested', put out to tender for private consortia to bid for. An 'in-house' team (the prison management, backed by the POA) was allowed to compete and won. The regime they have provided in the new gaol is exceptional for a British prison. Prisoners are out of their cells for 16 hours a day, have access to showers, phones, exercise, gym. There is work at a basic pay rate of £8 per week (compared to, for example, the £2.75 average at HMP Wymott at the time of the 1993 riot there). Night time 'bang-up' is at 9.30pm, probably the latest in any prison in the country.

The new prison is not a holiday camp – but it does offer basic humane conditions. This is an indisputable victory for those who stood up four years ago and blew the lid off the dustbin that was then Strangeways.

I and K wings of the old prison reopened in 1991, just nine months after the revolt. Conditions there are dire, as bad as or worse than before April 1990; there have been several suicides. This regime has been deliberately kept as harsh as possible so that the men gaoled there will be prepared to sacrifice their rights in order to leave. The first prisoners who were moved from I and K wings to the new gaol had to sign a 'compact', a practice strongly recommended by the Woolf Inquiry and certain to continue, promising to behave and work in a manner required by the regime. In return, the regime promises to treat them humanely.

The 'compact' is a cynical way of buying compliance. It is an agreement between two completely unequal parties. The prisoner promises to 'toe the line' in return for being treated with basic human dignity. The most iniquitous clause states that, on the sole word of one officer, privileges can be withdrawn for seven days and there is no appeal. The new prison has far better physical conditions than the old but is designed for maximum control with landings half the size of the old ones, gated off in the middle.

I and K wings continue to operate alongside the new wings. They serve as a reception centre and unofficial punishment block. They are the stick and the new wings are the carrot. In most gaols you may end up in the punishment block; in the new Strangeways you start there and work, or promise to work, your way upwards and onwards.

And there is another 'left-over' from the bad old days. What made Strangeways a hell-hole was not just the appalling conditions but the domination of a small group of power-crazed, brutal screws.

Some weeks ago, leaving the prison after a visit, I saw a prison officer I recognised, a big fat man who has thrown his size and weight about at Strangeways for many years. Everyone connected with Strangeways knows about Duffy; so why, in this new model prison, are his type still there?

The answer is because he's on security; he's one of the 'burglars', the men who 'spin' (search) the cells. 'Good screws' who search your cell do so with respect to the fact that you live there; it is your home; it is personal. The 'dogs' show no respect; they tip things up, tear photographs off walls etc. They do so to provoke whoever's cell they are searching and they often succeed. The protester will then be dragged down to the block, beaten and, if he is badly marked, charged with assault to justify the marks. ('Had to restrain him, Sir.')

The 'burglars' also form the nucleus of the 'heavy mob'. They are usually first on the scene when the alarm bell goes following the observation of a perceived incident. Most incidents are minor – two men merely slagging each other, for example, but these screws do not want consultation, only confrontation.

Which leaves only one question to the Prison Service, the Strangeways management and especially the POA: if you seriously expect prisoners and their supporters to believe your words about improving prison conditions, why do you continue to have the likes of Duffy on your landings? You know these bullies represent a totally different view from the one you publicly purport to hold. If you want to prove you are seriously committed to improving the lot of prisoners, do so by getting rid of them.

Appendix Two

British prisons: repression and resistance

The modern prison: capitalist punishment – Nicki Jameson and Trevor Rayne[3]

Every city has one; Britain sends more people there than any other European country, but prison as we know it is a relatively new innovation. Incarceration as a systematic and universal punishment began only with the Industrial Revolution. It sought to discipline the working class to accept the conditions capitalism determined for it. Consequently prison is also an instrument used to isolate and hammer working class leaders. Prison policy combines liberal reform, emphasised in stable times for capitalism, and vicious retribution, emphasised when crisis looms for the ruling class.

Emergent capitalism forced the means of production out of the hands of labour and enforced 'a degraded and almost servile condition of the mass of the people, their transformation into mercenaries and the transformation of their means of labour into capital' (*Marx*). From the Tudor period onwards a growing army of unattached proletarians was hurled onto the labour market by the dissolution of feudal retainers, abolition of monasteries and enclosure movement. Imprisonment and terroristic punishments were used to discipline this 'army of beggars, robbers and vagabonds' into acceptance of waged labour. During the 16th century land values increased and enclosures accelerated. The 1601 Poor Law established 'Bridewells' or 'Houses of Correction' to lock up petty criminals, vagrants and the poor in general, to teach them to lead more 'useful' lives by means of forced labour.

Crime...

By 1770 three-quarters of all agricultural land in England was owned by 4,000-5,000 aristocrats and gentry. Alongside the enclosures and accompanying dispossession of the rural populations there developed a new emphasis in the treatment of crime. Previously, offences against people were considered most serious – and the higher up in society the victim, the more serious the crime; the new serious crimes were committed against property. The range of capital offences increased so rapidly that criminal law became popularly known as the Bloody Code. Anything posing even a minor threat to the emerging rural landlord and capitalist classes, such as poaching or forgery, became a hanging matter.

The urban population swelled with the dispossessed. They were dangerous to the newly triumphant capitalism – poor, unintegrated, disrespectful and volatile. E P Thompson writes of the second half of the 18th century: 'One may even see these years as ones in which the class war is fought out in terms of Tyburn, the hulks and the Bridewells on the one hand; and crime, riot and mob action on the other.'

...and punishment

Following the 1789 French Revolution the ruling class lived in terror that the upheaval would spread to Britain. Public executions had become carnivals in which the condemned played the hero; the mere assembly of such large crowds at executions was seen as a danger. Similarly, punishments based on public humiliation, such as the stocks, fell from favour as the community could no longer be relied on to aim the rotten fruit, stones and insults at the intended victim, targeting the attendant magistrates instead!

Throughout the late 18th and early 19th centuries there were crime waves, part real, part imagined by a ruling class which lived in fear that 'the mob' would rise out of the sewers and destroy its property and privilege. Fear of crime and fear of political upheaval were conflated; 'the mob' and 'Jacobinism' became interchangeable bogeymen. The Wilkes Riots of the London 'mob' in the 1760s and '70s – in which the call for people's rights was mobilised in the interests of the City; the Gordon Riots of 1780, ostensibly against 'Popery', when London became a 'sea of fire'; these and countless other episodes revealed 'a groping desire to settle accounts with the rich, if only for one day'. (George Rudé, *Wilkes and liberty*)

The authorities felt powerless: they could not execute more people for fear of sparking even greater upheaval. Juries and magistrates, appalled by the severity of punishments they were expected to mete out, began refusing to convict or deliberately convicting on lesser charges. Even the prosecution would resist seeking the death penalty for small offenders; their consciences encouraged by fear of their houses being burned down.

Before the Industrial Revolution prison was primarily used to hold people before trial or punishment by ducking, flogging, disfiguration, the stocks, transportation or death. At the Old Bailey between 1770 and 1774 just 2.3 per cent of sentences were custodial; most were for weeks or months and the maximum was three years. 66.5 per cent of sentences were for transportation to the Americas for seven years, 14 years or life. The situation was brought to an acute crisis with the loss of the American colonies: between 1776 and 1786 there was a 73 per cent increase in the prison population; custodial sentences increased from 2.3 per cent to 28.6 per cent. The prisons experienced outbreaks of fever, riots and escapes, and the government was besieged by petitions from prisoners demanding release, transfer or improvement in conditions. The search for new methods of social control became urgent.

'Reform'

Under the twin banners of philanthropic reform and rational scientific progress, John Howard, author of *The State of the Prisons in England and Wales* (1777) and the namesake of today's Howard League for Penal Reform, set out to prove that 'There is a mode of managing some of the most desperate with ease to yourself and advantage to them. Shew them that you have humanity and that you aim to make them useful members of society.'

Howard toured the country's prisons and found convicted prisoners in chains, disease rife, richer inmates renting their own rooms while the poor slept in squalid dormitories. Visitors came and went bearing food; alcohol, sex (freely-given or purchased) and gambling were easily accessible. He evolved the idea of a 'penitentiary': silent, hygienic and austere, where criminals would live and work industriously on their own, uncontaminated literally and figuratively by contact with others. They would be retrained and re-educated to lead law-abiding lives and, through contemplation and religious instruction, feel guilt and remorse and so forsake crime.

Like all reformists, Howard and his contemporaries understood that excessive brutality and obvious injustice called into question the legitimacy of the entire system to a point where opposition of a revolutionary character might shake the very foundations of the established order.

Cold Bath Fields and Millbank

'As he went through Cold Bath Fields he saw a solitary cell;
And the devil was pleased, for it gave him a hint,
Of improving his prisons in Hell.'
Southey and Coleridge 'The Devil's Thoughts'

After the passing of the Penitentiary Act, drafted by Howard, Eden and Blackstone in 1779, there was a delay of over 30 years before the building of Millbank, Britain's first state prison, in 1812-16. Following the French Revolution, the ruling class did not want to be viewed as retreating from physical retribution or associating with ideas of reform and rehabilitation. However, new gaols were built under local auspices. The largest was Cold Bath Fields in Clerkenwell which opened in 1794. It contained a shot drill yard, where prisoners carried cannon balls up and down stairs, and six tread-wheel yards. A prisoner was expected to turn the wheel the equivalent of 12,000 feet of ascent a day. This regime so damaged the health of inmates that the Royal Artillery refused to send offenders there as they returned unfit for duty. Eventually the ascent distance was reduced to 1,200 feet per day.

When the Millbank finally opened it was Europe's largest prison, capable of holding 1,200 prisoners. The regime combined Howard's ideas of religious instruction, hard labour and solitary confinement, but was short-lived. Brutal gaolers and rebellious prisoners saw to that. Flogging was soon introduced and the gaol became overtly repressive. Prisoners were forbidden all reading material and their diet steadily reduced until, in 1823, 31 prisoners died of typhus, dysentery and scurvy and 400 were taken seriously ill.

Prisons were regularly targeted by the 'mob' and their inmates released. Similarly, on the inside, prisoners would rise up as at Gloucester prison in 1815, Millbank 1818 and 1826-27, Portland and Chatham 1861. In 1800 a protest by prisoners at Cold Bath Fields attracted massive support from the workers of Clerkenwell. They milled around the walls, shouting encouragement to the prisoners, who called down to the people to tear down the walls. Chants of 'Pull down the Bastille!' began to rise from the crowd, who were only dispersed by the combined forces of the Bow Street Runners and a hastily mobilised group of local property owners, the Clerkenwell Volunteers, using a cannon positioned in front of the prison gate.

Class struggle

As the ideas of Tom Paine and the French Revolution were taken up by the Radicals in Britain, so prisons were used to try and silence them. Stamp duty on publications and extended powers to prosecute 'sedition' resulted in many imprisonments. Richard Carlile continued to edit *The Republican* from gaol. He was supported by 150 volunteers who, between them, served 200 years of imprisonment in defiance of the law. Up to 750 people were prosecuted for 'unstamped' material between 1816 and 1836.

The Chartists, established in 1837-8, with their principal demand for universal adult male suffrage, had their leaders like Feargus O'Connor and Ernest Jones imprisoned. A Chartist-led revolt in 1842 resulted in 146 people being sentenced to prison with hard labour, in the Potteries alone. After the last great Chartist march in 1848, almost 500 were arrested and sentenced to terms of imprisonment.

By now imprisonment was the main punishment for all offenders (except those sentenced to death), together with the crank, the treadwheel and penal servitude. For the first time sentences over three years came into use along with the 'ticket-of-leave' system, the precursor of parole. Pentonville prison was built in 1842, using the 'panopticon' design, conceived by Jeremy Bentham, whereby a centrally placed observer could survey the whole prison, as wings radiated out from this position. Over the next six years 54 new prisons were built using the panopticon design, which was also employed for mills where a foreman could simultaneously oversee the whole workforce.

State power

In 1877 the prison system was unified into a single state-run service. Its first commissioner was Du Cane. He abolished integral sanitation and had all the toilets removed from Pentonville. Press and public were banned from setting foot in the prisons. Prisoners were required to face the wall when not in their cells or wear masks and maintain absolute silence. In this way they could not identify or recognise one another; nor could they organise. If they transgressed they were punished by being put in a pitch black cell, fed only bread and water and flogged.

As the system became entrenched, certain changes were made to it, usually under the cloak of 'reform'. The use of entirely dark cells was discontinued in 1884. Hard labour was partially abolished in 1898 in favour of 'productive labour' and abolished entirely in 1948 along with flogging, which ceased to be a punishment ordered by the courts but continued to be administered against inmates who assaulted prison staff until 1968. 'Separate confinement' was officially abolished in 1922 but the use of solitary confinement continues as a means of punishment for subversion to this day.

The Industrial Revolution stamped its marks on every town in Britain: the factory, the mill and the prison. But by building these institutions into which the proletariat was cast in ever increasing numbers, the conditions were also created for opposition: the factory and the mill had their strikes, the prison its riots. Few skylines are dominated today by Victorian mills and factories, yet the prisons still stand and new ones join them every year. They are still used to threaten, bully and isolate the working class; the balance between psychological and physical punishment is still tipped this way and that; the debate between different sections of the ruling class about whether the gaols are for reform or for punishment continues. And the objects of their deliberations still reject their treatment, still protest, still riot, still fight back. Thankfully.

The democratic spirit of Hull 1976 – Terry O'Halloran, Alexa Byrne, Beth Summer[4]

Mike Russell was within two months of finishing a five year prison sentence when Hull prison exploded. He was consequently to spend a further 16 months in prison.

Hull was considered a 'liberal' prison from 1968 to 1970. Significantly, very little use was made of solitary confinement and Rule 43. However, from 1970 rules were tightened. Discipline became 'stricter' – more oppressive, that is.

By 1975, Hull had the worst record of any dispersal prison for repression. In 1975 eight per cent of all 'offences' committed in dispersal prisons were committed in Hull. Yet Hull accounted for 40 per cent of all sentences of solitary confinement. In 1968 there were only nine solitary confinements given as punishments; in 1975 there were 122 – a more than 13-fold increase.

So when Artie Clifford was beaten on 31 August 1976 Hull prisoners had had enough. 'We decided,' said Mike Russell 'to have a peaceful protest.' Governor Kearns had departed just two weeks before, to be replaced by H Parr. Parr was, however, in the same mould. He refused to talk to the prisoners. 'He told us he wasn't going to be dictated to by "convicts, murderers and IRA terrorists." '

The prisoners formed their own elected committee. They decided to remain in the centre of the prison until Clifford was released. All the other prisoners were locked up. About 80 took part in the protest.

They were put in A wing. Very quickly the wing was wrecked. As Ray McLaughlin described it:

> '. . . that whole wing was wrecked from top to bottom . . . The release and frustration and anger and everything else, all the pent-up emotions in prison.'

The prisoners got through to the block and released Artie Clifford who bore visible marks of his beating. They freed all the prisoners in segregation. Paul Hill, one of the Guildford Four, described his feelings as he helped release the prisoners in solitary:

> 'I also felt and adored the feeling of how the cons down in the block hugged us as if we had just broken them from hell, some were so happy they even had tears in their eyes . . .'

At this stage, on the first day of the rising, there were still many prisoners unwilling to take part or undecided. It was then that prisoners captured the files held on them.

As Mike Russell said, 'once they saw the shit written about them,' the undecided prisoners joined in. 'One guy had a life sentence: "After 13 years this man is to be nutted off, never ever to get out of gaol"; he was married: "We must break up this man's marriage." '

The prisoners broke through to the roof and gained control of A, C and D wings. They held them for four days despite the drafting in of prison officers from all over the country. The prison was surrounded by armed police. Army vehicles and soldiers were seen outside the prison.

The divisions vanished. 'The strength of Hull was that everybody forgot their personal differences. What mattered was us and them. We elected a committee to negotiate.It was very democratic. Everyone could say their piece. All the demands were voted on.'

The prisoners negotiated with the Home Office. Their main demands were: restoration of privileges, no victimisation, no damage to property, right to see solicitors, a public inquiry. They also demanded that they surrender only to Hull prison officers – so that they could identify them in case of attack. Each prisoner was to be seen by an independent doctor. The Home Office agreed. On 3 September the prisoners ended the Hull rising in perfect discipline. Only one prison officer had been slightly hurt in the whole rising. The Home Office reneged on the agreement.

Within days the systematic beating of prisoners – especially Irish and black prisoners – began. Mike explains what happened to him:

'They kicked and banged on my door all night. "We're going to get you, you black bastard." The next morning when I had to slop out, I had to go through the gauntlet of screws. They kicked me, punched me up and down the landings three or four times. The screws shouted, "Come on. Niggers are good runners." '

The beating was repeated when Mike went to get his breakfast. Dozens of prisoners were viciously and repeatedly beaten while Assistant Governor A S Manning watched.

After the beatings came the adjudication. The Hull Board of Visitors handed out massive sentences of solitary and loss of remission – up to 720 days' loss of remission: equivalent to a prison sentence of nearly three years.

Mike described his own 'hearing' in which two different prison officers claimed to have seen him in two different places at the same time. Another officer's statement was used although the officer was not at the 'hearing' and could not be questioned.

Mike objected to such kangaroo court practices. 'I sat down and showed them my back. So they found me guilty on all charges.' He was given 480 days' loss of remission.

Thanks to the persistent work of PROP, the truth about the rising, particularly about the savage beatings, gradually emerged. After a delay of two years, 12 prison officers and Assistant Governor Manning were tried at York Crown Court in 1978. The AG and four prison officers were acquitted. The maximum sentence against the eight found guilty was nine months' imprisonment suspended. At the time of this trial, some prisoners were still serving their punishment from the uprising.

Despite the brutal revenge exacted by the prison authorities, the Hull prison rising remains a high point of prisoner resistance in Britain. Ray McLaughlin said:

'...a great comradeship built up between all prisoners, blacks, English, Irish, everybody...it was really international in a sense...It was really as if you were released from prison...'

The Risley trial – Jeremy Hawthorne[5]

Jubilant applause came from the dock as jurors delivered verdicts of Not Guilty. But greater praise is due to those who, having carried through a three-day protest, then had to survive a five-month trial.

They had faced impressive odds. Enormous damage was done to D Wing and they were there while it happened. Most were supposedly bang to rights in 36 hours of video. They were victims of identification procedures which broke all the rules of video evidence. Several were now serving long prison terms – so who would believe them?

Add to that the procedure. The prosecution obtained a 'voluntary bill of indictment', depriving the defence of using committal proceedings to test evidence in advance. The trial judge was renowned for hostility to defendants and for heavy sentencing. Trips to and from court were marked by tight and oppressive security measures.

Then the charge itself – riot, a charge never used in prison before. What did it mean, 'unlawful violence for a common purpose'? Defendants came under the heaviest pressure to plead Guilty, even from lawyers who said there was no defence.

Yet in a sense the Home Office had lost the battle before it started. 'Grisly Risley' had had an appalling reputation in Liverpool since the 1960s. HM Inspectorate reports of 1980 and 1988 were extremely critical. The spate of suicides was well-covered by local media. Even the official inquiry into this very incident (conveniently never published) made its number one recommendation that Risley should close.

How to make these diabolical conditions legally 'relevant'? As soon as the trial began it became clear the incident was not mindless damage but a protest for change. The main argument was that inmates could use 'reasonable force' as they were, so to speak, 'falsely imprisoned'.

It could also be said that inmates acted in 'self-defence'. When the riot bell went they were faced with an ill-ordered rabble of officers charging up the stairs with no overall control, varying levels of training and precious little idea of what they were doing. Shades of Hull '76, Scrubs '79 – would this be Risley '89? The only safe course was to 'barricade in' until safety could be guaranteed.

Over 70 prison officers gave evidence. Several were directly contradicted by the video. Once shown up, they began to admit racial abuse was rife at Risley. They admitted that 'unauthorised pyrotechnics' were brought in on 1 May and actually issued for use. They admitted hosing inmates on the first night. They admitted there was a plan the second day to retake D Wing by force. Many showed complete ignorance of suicide prevention. The governor made much of his great initiative to improve the atrocious diet : a pink 'supper bun' at 7pm each day!

To be fair, several officers agreed Risley was a dump and the ex-Regional Director Driscoll said he'd tried for four years to close it.

On video were the extensive negotiations between inmates and whoever was prepared to listen. Only on the third day did the authorities take the talks seriously: once that happened the protesters agreed conditions and a time for surrender and kept their bargain.

Clearly on both 'conditions' and 'negotiations', the prosecution were in trouble. But there remained 'Wadi 3', a report composed for *Fight Racism! Fight Imperialism!* by Wadi Williams at Hull prison and handed to the police by his course tutor. (Moral: free speech in prison can seriously damage your defence.) This was only 'evidence' against Williams but it was introduced to try to smear the entire protest and cause dissension among defendants. As it turned out though, even this tactic backfired. Wadi admitted a bit of 'journalistic licence' and this intensely readable rhapsody enlivened the tedium of the trial at just the right moment.

Ten defendants gave evidence and each had a different tale. It was obvious the grievances were too many to have been made up: conditions cried out for a protest and when it happened inmates had to protect themselves.

Even the best efforts of the judge could not convict anyone. He disallowed the defence of 'lawful protest' and made it clear he didn't believe the 'self-defence' argument. When the jury on their second day out asked for guidance he gave it and immediately eight were acquitted with a ninth let out later that day. Come the fifth day he volunteered more guidance, so biased as to leave even the jurors open-mouthed. Acquittals of the remaining 11 followed.

Time will tell whether the Home Office have learnt anything from this case. But even if they haven't, some of the general public have. If there is a single message it is that prisoners deserve more respect and better conditions. Prisoners everywhere can thank the Risley defendants for their courage and perseverance.

Wadi 3 – the inside story of the Risley uprising[6]

The now famous observation by Judge Tumim that Risley was 'barbarous and squalid' assumes terrifying substance when it is noted that six of the suicides in the last decade occurred in the last year, and that in a five week period in 1988 there were three suicides. This 'squalor and barbarism' was not limited purely to the carnage of inmate corpses but manifested itself in the filthy, inhuman squalor and putrid conditions which drove a great many of us to the fringes of suicide, when, that is, it did not drive us out of our minds completely.

It was the institutional callousness and environmental brutality which defined the texture of 'Gris Ris' and it is our collective refusal to tolerate this celebration of brutality and challenge and resist the culture and politics of 'barbarism and squalor' which define the events of 1-3 May 1989.

On 30 April (Sunday) there had been a disturbance in B wing over a host of issues (food, living conditions, etc). Despite the fact that D wing was not involved in this initial protest and is quite a long way from B wing, the MUFTI squad chose to make a show of force by marching into D wing at 11pm, banging on our cell doors, abusing all and sundry and parading up and down the landings until the early hours of Monday morning – clearly a deliberate act of provocation.

We in D wing, independently of B wing, had decided to commemorate 1 May by registering our displeasure with our condition of captivity and demonstrating our solidarity with the multitudes of dispossessed. Our intention was to conduct a peaceful 'sit-down' protest, to call attention to the nightmare of Risley in particular and our reality in general. The plan was to demand a public inquiry into Risley, present the Administration with a list of changes which required immediate implementation. We were even at this stage acutely aware of the need to conduct both an internal and public protest in order to bring this whole issue to the attention of both the Home Office and the general public. With this in mind, we intended, among other things, to demand access to the press.

At about 10am, we assembled in the caged exercise yard to start our protest. However, it soon became clear that the MUFTI squad was lurking in the connecting corridor, while dog handlers were gathering on the other side of the fences. Clearly a sit-down protest on the exercise yard would have left us open to a dual attack from the MUFTI and the dogs. We therefore decided to transfer the protest indoors to one of the landings. We reasoned that given the limited access, if the Administration decided to attack, it was a defendable position.

Over 120 inmates assembled on landing Five which usually housed 30-40. Before dialogue could be opened, the screws present simply looked around and contemptuously told us to 'get behind our doors'. This contemptuous dismissal of our peaceful protest was the trigger which finally ignited the uprising. Someone threw a cup; the screws then hit the alarm/riot bell and bolted from the landing.

With the MUFTI on the ground floor corridor rushing up the stairs we had a serious head-on confrontation – we were seriously concerned for our safety, given the squad's reputation for gross violence and brutality. We were faced with the stark choice of either waiting passively to be brutalised and violated or resisting and defending ourselves by any means necessary. We took the latter course.

We quickly began to fashion a barricade and the struggle for control of the wing was on. We were obliged to confront the staves and shields of the MUFTI with whatever was immediately to hand. This included pouring concentrated liquid soap down the stairs to prevent them rushing up the stairwell; doors were taken off their hinges and used to barricade the main access area. All this, while some of us were engaged in hand-to-hand combat for control of the landing. After 10-15 minutes of fierce combat we secured control of landing Five and then turned our attention to landing Six. To gain access we had to breach a wall (this we did using a cell door). With our control of landings Five and Six we all but had internal control of D wing, however we were still vulnerable to possible counter-attacks via the main and flat roofs of D wing. In fact there was a race between us and the MUFTI as to who would gain control of the flat roof connecting the wing. Again, by using the steel cell doors with a relay of eight inmates we were able to blast our way through one of the main walls, enabling us to gain access to the flat roof, just as the MUFTI were assembling to storm the area. There then ensued a brief but fierce struggle, after which they retreated and we were able to establish our defensive line and take control of the main roof and effectively take control of D wing. . . the uprising was now in full swing!

In the course of the struggle for D wing, it became clear that only a full scale protest and uprising could bring the whole issue to the public's attention and ensure that we are included in the social and political agenda. In short, with our actions we wanted to fashion an eloquent political and social statement which went beyond the confines of prison and as such, (in addition to our public statement, registering our profound displeasure and anger, articulating our position vis à vis the need for change and a public inquiry) it became crucial that we hold on to D wing for at least 72 hours and then only call that stage of the uprising to a close, when and only when we felt the time was right and our basic conditions had been met. As a result, for the next 72 hours, we were engaged in almost continuous skirmishes, during which we overcame and repelled assaults ranging from midnight attacks with high-pressure water hoses (which nearly blew some of us off the roof) to sneak night-time attacks. Suffice to say we were able to resist all these assaults.

During the uprising we were also resolved to conduct ourselves in a most democratic/isocratic manner. So we arranged to have frequent mass assemblies which we all attended (apart from those on guard duty) and during which all salient issues were discussed and voted on, thus avoiding the pitfalls of creating a cabal of leaders. In our assemblies we discussed and determined strategies from food distribution, sleeping rota, guard duties, defence, honing our demands and negotiation position, to determining our response to the Home Office proposals. We also decided to invite all those who were not sure they wished to continue the struggle to leave, and over a 24-hour period we were able to persuade the waverers, or at least those who no longer had the stomach for the fight to leave... and thus was born... *The Risley 54 — We who were totally committed to the uprising.*

On 3 May after long, protracted and complex discussions and negotiations with representatives of the State (the Home Office) our demands were met and that stage of the uprising was brought to a close. We were subsequently charged with two counts of Riot and Criminal Damage – which carry a combined tariff of 20 years imprisonment.

It is no exaggeration to say that the Risley Uprising contained profound lessons which carry great relevance and significance for the wider struggle. For example, that in the crucible of struggle, capital and the state's ploy of divide and rule along racial lines can be successfully subverted. Despite explicit attempts by some screws to fracture our collective solidarity and struggle by shouting, 'Throw the niggers off the roof' and 'How can you be led by niggers?' etc, we held firm. And to this extent, the Risley 54 made a profound anti-racist statement and affirmed the 'triumph of the human spirit'. Unquestionably the uprising struck a powerful blow in support of the struggle against racism.

Furthermore, the Risley Uprising was an eloquent and elegant demonstration of the power and cohesive force of a truly egalitarian/isocratic organisation. We functioned and held together in the most difficult of circumstances, in no small measure because we took a conscious decision to 'avoid the pitfalls' of rigid formal leadership. Instead we subjected all relevant decisions to mass discussion and debate, from which a consensus or majority verdict emerged. In this way both responsibility and power were equally and equitably distributed. It is amazing the awesome creative strength this released in people whom 'society' had for so long dismissed as irrelevant.

Finally the Risley Uprising also demonstrated that the 'human spirit' remains *Unbroken! Unbowed!* and *Untwisted! Salud!*

Control and Restraint – Terry O'Halloran[7]

The Home Office Prison Department (now calling itself the Prison Service) is planning a crackdown in the guise of phasing out MUFTI (Minimum Use of Force Tactical Intervention) squads. The plans are revealed in a secret internal Prison Service circular.

The Circular, CI 58/1988, issued on 17 November 1988, is called 'The control of violent and recalcitrant inmates'. It is intended 'to improve the Service's state of pre-paredness to deal with inmate violence, and changes in techniques to deal with vio-lence on a large scale'.

As usual there is some introductory guff about the need to 'contain and manage dif-ficult, recalcitrant or violent behaviour by persuasion and other means which do not entail the use of force'. Notice how 'difficult' and 'recalcitrant' behaviour is treated as synonymous with 'violent' behaviour. Is a prisoner who insists on his or her rights 'difficult'? Is a prisoner who refuses to submit to arbitrary and illegal behaviour 'recalcitrant'?

Read on for an answer. 'The use of force must continue always to be regarded as a matter of last resort, whether staff are confronted with a passive demonstration, non-violent resistance, or acts of violence whether by individuals or groups acting in con-cert.' Again violent and non-violent protest are lumped together. What 'last resort' justified the use of systematic violence, resulting in more than 60 prisoners being injured, to break up the passive demonstration in Wormwood Scrubs 1979 – the first admitted use of the MUFTI squads?

The circular then tells us that 'situations sometimes arise in which the use of force is necessary in order to prevent an inmate injuring himself, other inmates or staff, or damaging property and in *certain circumstances to achieve compliance with prison discipline when other methods have failed or are inappropriate*' [emphasis added]. There you have it. The Home Office is telling prison staff that they can use force to 'achieve compliance with prison discipline'.

Now it is clear why 'difficult' and 'violent' behaviour are blurred together. To obscure the illegal character of the Home Office's advice. The law only gives prison officers the right to use such force as is reasonably necessary to prevent the commis-sion of a crime. The Home Office makes no reference to the law. Instead, it says: 'In such circumstances no more force must be used than is necessary to deal with the par-ticular situation'. The same thinking is enshrined in the Prison Rules.

Having established what it laughingly calls 'general principles', the circular gets down to business. Since 1984 prison officers have been trained in C&R (Control and Restraint). C&R 1 covers restraint of an individual prisoner or breaking up a fight and teams of three to disarm and/or remove a prisoner from a cell. C&R 2 covers self-defence techniques and teams of 12 to deal with a 'disturbance by a group'. The next stage, up to now, has been bringing in the MUFTI squads.

MUFTI now, however, is to be replaced by C&R 3. C&R 3 is based on teams of 36 (three teams of twelve) who will have 'newer-style helmets, flame-retardant suits', 'shields', 'protective gloves, shin/knee guards' and 'specialist protective boots'. Male officers will have new 'side-arm batons' and female officers will have 'kubotans'. Kubotans are the type of batons used by US and Canadian police with a handle projecting at right angles.

All officers will be trained in C&R 1 and C&R 2 self-defence. 'A body of officers' in each prison will be trained in C&R 2 teams of 12 and C&R 3. Over 4,000 officers will be trained in C&R 3. This is far more than the numbers involved in MUFTI. This target is to be achieved by 31 March 1990.

In short MUFTI is to be replaced by a bigger, better trained, better equipped riot squad with a unit in every prison. As is always the case with Home Office doublespeak, phase out means crackdown. Prisoners and their supporters have to act now to prepare for this next phase of repression.

1. *Fight Racism! Fight Imperialism!* 107 June/July 1992.
2. *Fight Racism! Fight Imperialism!* 118 April/May 1994.
3. *Fight Racism! Fight Imperialism!* 119 June/July 1994.
4. *Fight Racism! Fight Imperialism!* 62 September 1986. Sources: *Don't Mark His Face* – PROP; interview with Ray McLaughlin in *Fight Racism! Fight Imperialism!* 41; interview with Mike Russell. Another excellent description of the Hull uprising is contained in Ray McLaughlin's book *Inside an English Jail*.
5. *Fight Racism! Fight Imperialism!* 98 December 1990/January 1991. Jeremy Hawthorne was solicitor to Wadi Williams, the number one accused in the Risley trial.
6. ibid.
7. 'Home Office to crack down in prisons' *Fight Racism! Fight Imperialism!* 83 January 1989.

Chronology

SUNDAY 1 APRIL 1990
Protest begins in Strangeways chapel and spreads through rest of prison

Hull – roof-top protest and sit-in in exercise yard
Minor protests at Kirkham and Rochester

MONDAY 2 APRIL
Papers report 12-20 dead, kangaroo courts, castrations, hangings
Prisoners display banner: *No Dead*
140 prisoners hold five wings of prison

Long Lartin – escape attempt and protest
Small scale protests at Lindholme, Bedford and Low Newton

TUESDAY 3 APRIL
Prisoners' banner reads: *Media contact now*
Michael Unger goes into gaol as 'independent' observer
Derek White, remanded on Rule 43, dies in hospital from injuries sustained on Sunday 1st
35 prisoners surrender
Tabloids continue to run '20-30 dead' stories

WEDNESDAY 4 APRIL
Governor Brendan O'Friel makes 'explosion of evil' statement

29 prisoners surrender; 26 remain

Durham – prison officer taken hostage
Minor protests at Winchester, Wandsworth, Full Sutton, Stafford and Brockhill

THURSDAY 5 APRIL
Home Office announces Woolf Inquiry and says that all sex-offenders and Cat A prisoners are accounted for
Tony Bush and John Spencer surrender

FRIDAY 6 APRIL
Andrew Nelson and Mark Petrie surrender
Police use loud music to try and force prisoners down

Glen Parva – 'disturbance' involving 50 young prisoners

SATURDAY - SUNDAY 7-8 APRIL
O'Friel says he 'cannot rule out bodies'
Horfield, Bristol – 400 prisoners take over three wings of prison
Dartmoor – 100-120 prisoners in large-scale protest; 12 on roof
Armley – sit-down protest
Cardiff – 130 prisoners destroy cells and surrounding areas for three hours

Stoke Heath – 20-hour occupation of A wing roof
Hull – 110 prisoners stage second sit-in in exercise yard
Other incidents at Brixton, Shepton-Mallet, Pentonville, Canterbury and Stafford

MONDAY 9 APRIL

The Verne – windows smashed
Bristol – recaptured
Dartmoor – one man, Joseph Collins, still on roof
Everthorpe – 65 prisoners barricade themselves in for three hours

TUESDAY 10 APRIL

13 prisoners remain at Strangeways

Shotts – 40 prisoners take over B Hall and hold prison officer hostage for 24 hours

WEDNESDAY 11 APRIL

Barry Morton, Mark Azzopardi and Nathan Gaynor surrender

Dartmoor – four prisoners stage rooftop protest

THURSDAY 12 APRIL

Swansea – two teenage remand prisoners barricade themselves in their cell for 17 hours

FRIDAY 13 APRIL

Press Council inquiry into coverage announced

SATURDAY 14 APRIL

Dartmoor – Joseph Collins surrenders

SUNDAY 15 APRIL

Strangeways central rotunda on fire

MONDAY 16 APRIL

Iain McKinlay, Kevin Gee and Earl Fahey surrender with food-poisoning; seven prisoners remain

TUESDAY 17 APRIL

Prisoners negotiate with authorities for end to siege

WEDNESDAY 18 APRIL

Prisoners eat breakfast on roof and shower in the water spray.
Robert Litherland MP visits gaol

THURSDAY 19 APRIL

O'Friel finally says 'no dead'

FRIDAY 20 APRIL

Greater Manchester police ask for £2m for policing costs

SUNDAY 22 APRIL

David Waddington visits Strangeways

Pucklechurch – 100 remand prisoners aged 17-21 begin protest
Two prisoners stage four-hour roof-top protest at Winson Green

MONDAY 23 APRIL

Alan Lord is snatched on his way to negotiate

Pucklechurch – siege ended by force

TUESDAY 24 APRIL

Strangeways has biggest fires so far
Lily Taylor arrested

Full Sutton – 400 prisoners confined to cells as part of 'weapons and drugs search'

WEDNESDAY 25 APRIL

Darren Jones snatched – 10.20am
Final five surrender – 6.20pm

During the 25 days of the Strangeways protest there were also small-scale protests at the following prisons: Deerbolt, Wymott, Castington, Portland, Liverpool, Kirklevington, Gloucester and Camp Hill.

WOOLF INQUIRY

11-29 June 1990 — Woolf Inquiry opens at the Freemasons' Hall in Manchester, to hear evidence about events at Strangeways,
9-23 July — Inquiry at Taunton re Bristol, Dartmoor, Bristol and Cardiff
31 July - 1 August — London re Glen Parva
26 September — Seminars start in London
31 October — Woolf Inquiry finishes hearing evidence in public
25 February 1991 — Report published

September 1991 — White Paper *Custody, Care and Justice* published

TRIALS

14 January-16 April 1992: Paul Taylor, Alan Lord, 'Tiny' Doran, Martin McLatchie, Nicholas Webb, Andrew Nelson, Jimmy Miller, Brian Parke, John Spencer — Riot and Murder,

5 October 1992-1 March 1993 — Alan Lord, Kevin Gee, Glyn Williams, Tony Bush, David Bowen, Barry Morton, Mark Azzopardi, Mark Williams, Nathan Gaynor, John Murray, Martin Brian, Earl Fahey, Andrew Nelson, Darren Jones — Conspiracy to commit GBH with intent.

Glossary

MUFTI – Minimum Use of Force Tactical Intervention (Riot squad 1979-1990)
C&R – Control and Restraint (Riot squad 1990 onwards)

BOV – Board of Visitors
PO – prison officer
SO – senior officer
YP – Young prisoner

Lay-down – punitive administrative transfer to another gaol for a 28-day 'cooling-off' period.

GOAD – Good Order and Discipline: Segregation under Prison Rule 43(b); (Rule 43(a) is used to segregate prisoners 'for their own protection')

Seg/Seg unit/block – punishment wing of prison where prisoners are held in isolation from the rest of the prison population.

Bibliography

On the Strangeways prison protest:

REPORTS AND OFFICIAL PUBLICATIONS:

Custody, Care and Justice: the Way Ahead for the Prison Service in England and Wales HMSO 1991.

Partners of Prisoners Support, *Report of the Strangeways Family Crisis Centre during Riots April 1990*.

The Press Council, *Press at the Prison Gates* 1991.

Report by HM Chief Inspector of Prisons, HM Prison Manchester Home Office 1990.

Woolf, The Rt Hon Lord Justice and Tumim, His Honour Judge Stephen, *Prison Disturbances April 1990 Report of an Inquiry*, HMSO 1991.

NEWSPAPERS:

Fight Racism! Fight Imperialism! 95, 96, 98, 100, 107, 108, 110, 111, 118.

Taking Liberties and *ABC Newsletter* (publications of the Anarchist Black Cross) 1991-3.

Daily Express 7 April 1990.

Daily Mirror 3, 4 April 1990.

Daily Star 4, 24 April 1990.

The Daily Telegraph 3, 26 April 1990.

The Guardian 2-26 April 1990, 26 February 1991.

The Independent 5, 26 April 1990.

Manchester Evening News 2-25 April 1990, 27 May 1994.

The Observer 8 April 1990.

The Sun 3, 5, 6, 9 April 1990.

The Times 3 April 1990.

On the prison system (primary sources):

Coggan, Geoff and Walker, Martin, *Frightened for my life* Fontana 1982.
Fight Racism! Fight Imperialism! Issues 45, 62, 83, 98, 115, 119, 120.
Hands Off Ireland! Number 9. RCG Publications Ltd 1979.
Ignatieff, Michael, *A Just Measure of Pain – the penitentiary in the industrial revolution 1750-1850* Penguin 1989 (first published 1978).
McLaughlin, Raymond, *Inside an English Jail* Borderline 1987.
Prison Service *Corporate Plan* 1994-97
Stern, Vivien, *Bricks of Shame – Britain's Prisons* Penguin. Second Edition (Revised) 1989.

On the prison system (secondary sources):

Abbott, Jack Henry, *In the belly of the beast* Hutchinson, 1981.
Bean, J P, *Over the wall* Headline 1994.
Davis, Angela, *If they come in the morning…* Orbach and Chambers 1971.
Drummond-Murray, James, 'Mount Pleasant Post Office: an archeological assessment' Museum of London Archaeology Service. Unpublished Report 1992.
Fitzgerald, Mike and Sim, Joe, *British Prisons* Blackwells 1979.
Foucault, Michel, *Discipline and Punish – the birth of the prison (Surveiller et punir)* Penguin 1977.
Hercules, Trevor, *Labelled a black villain* Fourth Estate 1989.
Hughes, Robert, *Fatal Shore* Pan 1988.
Jackson, George, *Blood in my eye* Penguin 1972.
Jackson, George, *Soledad Brother* Jonathan Cape and Penguin 1971.
Lytton, Constance, *Prisons and Prisoners* Heinemann 1918, Virago 1988.
McKinlay, Paul, *Scottish Prisons – Lift the lid* Larkin Publications 1986.
O'Donovan Rossa, Jeremiah, *Irish Rebels in English Prisons* Brandon 1991 (first published 1872).
Peterson, Mickey, *The Liquid Cosh* Breakout Collective 1984.
Priestley, Philip, *Jail Journeys* Routledge 1989.
Ross, Paul and Jakubczyk, Andrzy, *One-off* 1992. (This publication can be obtained from Chas Wilson, School of Social and Historical Studies, University of Portsmouth, Milldam, Burnaby Road, Portsmouth PO1 3AS. Price £3.)
Sim, Joe, *Medical Power in Prisons* Open University Press 1990.
Smith, Ken, *Inside Time* Harrap 1989.
Stratton, Brian, *Who Guards the Guards?* PROP 1973 (Third Edition).
Thompson, E P, *The Making of the English Working Class*
Watson, Bruce, 'The Compter Prisons of London', *London Archaeologist* vol 7 no 5 pp115-121, Winter 1993.
Wilde, Oscar, *The Ballad of Reading Gaol* 1898.

Index

Also available from Larkin Publications in the Counterattack Series:

Subscribe now to
FIGHT RACISM!
FIGHT IMPERIALISM!

– the only newspaper which consistently supports the struggles of prisoners.

For the past 15 years *Fight Racism! Fight Imperialism!* has reported on the struggle by prisoners against the inhumanities of the British prison system. Every issue of the paper contains at least one 'Prisoners' Fightback' page and a large proportion of the material is written by prisoners who read FRFI. Coverage is not restricted to factual reporting but also includes debates on issues such as prison privatisation and prisoners' rights.

Among left-wing newspapers in Britain, FRFI is unique in its support for prisoners. The paper is sent free of charge to 200 prisoners and avidly read by many more.

Subscribe to FRFI now!

Subscription rates:
Britain (inc N. Ireland): £5 for 6 issues, £9.50 for 12 issues
EC/Europe air printed paper rate: £6.50 for six issues, £12.50 for 12 issues
Africa, America, Middle East, South Asia printed paper rate: £9.50 for six issues, £18 for 12 issues.
East Asia, Australasia, Pacific air printed paper rate: £10 for 6 issues, £19.50 for 12 issues.
Libraries and institutions double individual rates.
Gift subscriptions for prisoners (recorded): £7 for six issues, £13 for 12 issues.
I would like to subscribe to FRFI for _____ issues and enclose _____

I would like to pay for an additional subscription for a prisoner and enclose_____

(Please make cheques and POs payable to Larkin Publications)

Name _____

Address_____

_____

_____

Return to Larkin Publications, BCM Box 5909, London WC1N 3XX.

TERRY O'HALLORAN MEMORIAL FUND

The fund was set up to honour the memory of
Terry O'Halloran (1952-1989)
a communist and fighter for Irish freedom
and prisoners' rights.

The Memorial Fund supplies books and subscriptions
to prisoners who are unable to afford them
themselves.

If you are a prisoner and wish to receive a book please
write to the address below.

If you would like to support the fund by a donation or
gift of books, please contact us at the address below

**Terry O'Halloran Memorial Fund
BCM Box 5960, London WCIN 3XX**